I'm blown away by this book and excited to add
The authors have managed to compose a thoroughly referenced encyclopedic treatise of the study of organizational change that is engagingly readable, relatable, and accessible. I am confident this will become the go-to reference source for both graduate students and seasoned professionals. It illuminates the various levers for change, as well as how consulting psychologists can facilitate change at the individual, organizational, and, most importantly, systemic levels. From the classics of consulting psychology forward, Leonard, Kilburg, and Freedman have found the red thread that connects a century of work in our field. These psychologists have done a great job, and this is a fitting legacy to the lifelong work of the late Arthur Freedman.

—**Randall P. White, PhD,** Fellow, Division 13, American Psychological Association; Past President, Division 13, American Psychological Association; Founding Partner, Executive Development Group, Professor of Leadership, HEC Paris, Jouy-en-Josas, France

Celebrated consultants and mentors Leonard, Kilburg, and Freedman put it all together in one highly readable and fascinating book. Where do our organizational change models come from? How are they used today? I was excited to delve into diverse topics like covert processes in organizational change (aka psychodynamics), leading radical change, and action learning. You can pick and choose what you want to learn about and where you can take a deeper dive. An A+ experience!

—**Rebecca Turner, PhD,** Owner, Turner Consulting Group, San Francisco, CA, United States; Professor Emerita, California School of Professional Psychology

This book is a must-read for all psychologists who consult to organizational leaders, as well as for nonpsychologist organizational consultants and leadership coaches, and anyone else interested in better understanding psychological and change dynamics of organizational systems. This essential primer neatly knits together the philosophical and historical roots and key elements of the psychological science foundation supporting organizational systems change consulting, enhanced with examples of strategic approaches for guiding successful change. Kudos to the authors for this valuable contribution to consulting psychology.

—**Vicki V. Vandaveer, PhD,** International Organizational Consulting and Coaching Psychologist; Fellow of the American Psychological Association, Society of Consulting Psychology, Society of Industrial and Organizational Psychology; and Fellow of the International Society for Coaching Psychology

Essential Strategies for Organizational and Systems Change

Fundamentals of Consulting Psychology Book Series

Assessing CEOs and Senior Leaders: A Primer for Consultants
J. Ross Blankenship

Coaching Psychology: Catalyzing Excellence in Organizational Leadership
Vicki V. Vandaveer and Michael H. Frisch

Consulting Psychology in National Security Organizations
Laurie B. Moret and Carroll H. Greene III

Consulting to Technical Leaders, Teams, and Organizations: Building Leadership in STEM Environments
Joanie B. Connell

Essential Strategies for Organizational and Systems Change: An Overview for Consultants
H. Skipton Leonard, Richard R. Kilburg, and Arthur M. Freedman

The Ethical Practice of Consulting Psychology
Rodney L. Lowman and Stewart E. Cooper

Forensic Organizational Consulting: The Role of Psychologists in Litigation Support
Jay M. Finkelman with Linda Gomberg

An Introduction to Consulting Psychology: Working With Individuals, Groups, and Organizations
Rodney L. Lowman

Learning Interventions for Consultants: Building the Talent That Drives Business
Manuel London and Thomas Diamante

Transcultural Competence: Navigating Cultural Differences in the Global Community
Jerry Glover and Harris L. Friedman

Using Feedback in Organizational Consulting
Jane Brodie Gregory and Paul E. Levy

APA FUNDAMENTALS OF CONSULTING PSYCHOLOGY

Essential Strategies for Organizational and Systems Change

AN OVERVIEW FOR CONSULTANTS

H. SKIPTON LEONARD, RICHARD R. KILBURG,
AND ARTHUR M. FREEDMAN

AMERICAN PSYCHOLOGICAL ASSOCIATION

Published by
American Psychological Association
750 First Street, NE
Washington, DC 20002
https://www.apa.org

Order Department
https://www.apa.org/pubs/books
order@apa.org

In the U.K., Europe, Africa, and the Middle East, copies may be ordered from Eurospan
https://www.eurospanbookstore.com/apa
info@eurospangroup.com

Typeset in Minion by Circle Graphics, Inc., Reisterstown, MD

Printer: Gasch Printing, Odenton, MD
Cover Designer: Mark Karis

Library of Congress Cataloging-in-Publication Data

Names: Leonard, H. Skipton, author. | Kilburg, Richard R., 1946- author. | Freedman, Arthur M., author.
Title: Essential strategies for organizational and systems change : an overview for consultants / H. Skipton Leonard, Richard R. Kilburg, and Arthur M. Freedman.
Description: Washington, DC : American Psychological Association, [2023] | Series: Fundamentals of consulting psychology | Includes bibliographical references and index.
Identifiers: LCCN 2022024882 (print) | LCCN 2022024883 (ebook) | ISBN 9781433837876 (paperback) | ISBN 9781433837883 (ebook)
Subjects: LCSH: Organizational change. | Organizational behavior. | Business consultants. | BISAC: PSYCHOLOGY / Industrial & Organizational Psychology | BUSINESS & ECONOMICS / Consulting
Classification: LCC HD58.8 .L466 2022 (print) | LCC HD58.8 (ebook) | DDC 658.4/06--dc23/eng/20220526
LC record available at https://lccn.loc.gov/2022024882
LC ebook record available at https://lccn.loc.gov/2022024883

https://doi.org/10.1037/0000328-000

Printed in the United States of America

10 9 8 7 6 5 4 3 2 1

Contents

Series Editor's Foreword

Rodney L. Lowman

The field of consulting psychology has blossomed in recent years. It covers the applications of psychology in consulting to individuals, teams, organizations, and systems. Unfortunately, there are very few graduate training programs in this field of specialization, so consulting psychology roles are mostly populated by those who came to consulting psychology after having trained in other areas of psychology—including industrial and organizational (I/O), clinical/counseling, and school psychology, among others. Yet such training is rarely focused on consulting psychology and psychologists, and graduate students therefore have to learn the needed skills through on-the-job training, reading books and articles, attending conferences and workshops, and being mentored in the foundational competencies of the field as they seek to transition into it.

After a number of years of editing *Consulting Psychology Journal: Practice and Research*, the field's flagship journal, I felt that an additional type of educational product was needed to help those transitioning into consulting psychology. The Society of Consulting Psychology therefore partnered with the American Psychological Association to develop a new book series. The idea was to create a series of monographs on specific foundational skill sets needed to practice in this area of specialization. Working with an editorial advisory board, consisting of Drs. Judith Blanton, Brodie Gregory, Skipton Leonard (and initially Dale Fuqua and the late Edward Pavur, Jr.), and myself, our goal in the series has been to identify the major competencies needed by consulting psychologists and then to work with highly experienced authors to create short, accessible, evidence-based texts that would be useful both as stand-alone volumes and in combination with one another. The readers would be graduate students in relevant training programs, psychologists planning a transition into consulting psychology, and practicing professionals who want to add to their areas of expertise.

What are the fundamental skills needed in consulting psychology practice? The following sources provide useful starting points:

- *Guidelines for Education and Training at the Doctoral and Post-doctoral Level in Consulting Psychology (CP)/Organizational Consulting Psychology (OCP)*, created by the Society of Consulting Psychology and approved by the American Psychological Association in 2017 (Gullette et al., 2019)
- *Handbook of Organizational Consulting Psychology* (Lowman, 2002)
- *An Introduction to Consulting Psychology: Working With Individuals, Groups, and Organizations* (Lowman, 2016)

Each of these contributions was organized around the concept of levels (individual, group, and organizational) as a taxonomy for identifying fundamental skills. Within and across each of those categories, two broad skill sets are needed: assessment and intervention.

As with many areas of psychological practice, the foundational skills that apply in one area can overlap into others in the taxonomy. Interventions with individuals, as in executive coaching, for instance, usually take place in the context of work with a specific team and within specific organizations, which themselves also constitute a type of "client" (Schein, 1999).

Understanding the systemwide issues and dynamics at the organizational level usually also involves consulting activities with specific executives and teams, and multicultural/international issues suffuse many of our roles. The APA Guidelines (Gullette et al., 2019) and the *Handbook* (Lowman, 2016) concluded, properly, that consulting psychologists need to be trained in and have, at least, foundational skills and experience at the individual, group, and organizational levels, even if they primarily specialize in one of these areas.

In inviting you to learn more about consulting psychology through this book series, I hope you will come to agree that it is an exciting and inherently interesting area of study, research, and professional practice. The series aims not just to cover relevant literature on specific topics in consulting psychology but also to capture the richness of this work by including case material that illustrates its applications. Readers will soon understand that consulting psychologists are real-world activists, energized by the opportunity to work in, and to have a positive impact on, real-world environments. And in a world where organizations and the individuals and teams within them greatly need help in functioning ethically and effectively, in bridging individual, group, and organization-level needs and constituencies, and in coping with the rapid expansion of knowledge and escalating competition and internationalization, this book series aims to make a difference by helping more psychologists join the ranks of qualified consulting psychologists. Collectively, we can have a positive impact not just on an area of specialization in psychology but also on the world.

ABOUT THIS BOOK

This book was written by three highly experienced and well-published consulting psychologists. It is the first book in the series that focuses on organizational systems assessments and interventions.

Each of these three authors has had extensive experience working at the individual, team, and systems levels. Skipton Leonard has been a major contributor to the consulting psychology and action learning literature (e.g., Leonard, 2013; Leonard & Marquardt, 2010). He has worked in a variety of consulting roles, including as a senior leader in a national consulting firm. Richard Kilburg has written extensively on executive coaching and on the psychology of leaders (e.g., Kilburg, 2012; Kilburg & Dietrich, 2007). He has applied his expertise in a wide assortment of organizations, including corporations, health care systems, and universities.

Sadly, the third author, Arthur Freedman, died before this book was published. His contributions to the book are well-crafted and reflect the wisdom of a senior scholar and practitioner at the apex of his career. Arthur published more than 120 books, articles, and chapters and gave even more presentations. One of his books (whose coauthors include the first author of this book; Marquardt et al., 2009) illustrates the blend of theory and practice that Arthur embraced throughout his career. But, like the other two authors of the book, he was also a practitioner. His clients included advertising firms, breweries, conglomerates, consulting firms, broadcasting companies, professional associations, and many more. Additionally, he was present at the creation of the influential National Training Laboratories. I am pleased that his final work appears in this book.

As for the book's content, it aims to provide a broad overview of the theory and practice of organizational-level consulting. It introduces many concepts that apply primarily to organizational/systemic levels but also considers the role of groups and individuals to system-level consultation. The authors suggest, for example, that individual-level interventions with high-level executives can themselves be system-level interventions. Readers will find overviews of various topics that will orient them to the complexities that arise when assessing and intervening when consulting to organizations. The case material makes the theories and approaches come alive. The book provides a panoply of ideas and approaches useful to organizational consultants from many areas of specialization and levels of experience.

REFERENCES

Gullette, E. C. D., Fennig, J., Reynolds, T., Humphrey, C., Kinser, M., & Doverspike, D. (2019). Guidelines for education and training at the doctoral and postdoctoral levels in consulting psychology/organizational consulting psychology: Executive summary of the 2017 revision. *American Psychologist, 74*(5), 608–614. https://doi.org/10.1037/amp0000462

Kilburg, R. R. (2012). *Virtuous leaders: Strategy, character, and influence in the 21st century.* American Psychological Association. https://doi.org/10.1037/13494-000

Kilburg, R. R., & Dietrich, R. C. (Eds.). (2007). *The wisdom of coaching: Essential papers in consulting psychology for a world of change.* American Psychological Association.

Leonard, H. S. (2013). The history and current status of organizational and systems change theory. In H. S. Leonard, R. Lewis, A. M. Freedman, & J. Passmore (Eds.), *The Wiley-Blackwell handbook of the psychology of leadership, change & OD* (pp. 237–266). Wiley-Blackwell.

Leonard, H. S., & Marquardt, M. J. (2010). The evidence for the effectiveness of action learning. *Action Learning: Research and Practice*, *7*(2), 121–136. https://doi.org/10.1080/14767333.2010.488323

Lowman, R. L. (Ed.). (2002). *Handbook of organizational consulting psychology. A comprehensive guide to theories, skills, and techniques.* Jossey-Bass.

Lowman, R. L. (2016). *An introduction to consulting psychology: Working with individuals, groups, and organizations*. American Psychological Association. https://doi.org/10.1037/14853-000

Marquardt, M., Leonard, S., Freedman, A. M., & Hill, C. (2009). *Action learning for developing leaders and organizations: Principles, strategies, and cases.* American Psychological Association. https://doi.org/10.1037/11874-000

Schein, E. H. (1999). *Process consultation revisited: Building the helping relationship.* Addison-Wesley.

Dedication and Acknowledgments

DEDICATION TO ARTHUR M. FREEDMAN

This book is dedicated to Arthur M. Freedman in recognition and honor of his contributions to the fields of organization change and development and consulting psychology. Arthur integrated his early training in business and organizational management (MBA, Boston University) with a deep interest in personal and social change (PhD in clinical psychology, University of Chicago). He was an influential thought leader in social and organizational change for more than 50 years through his involvement with the National Training Laboratories, the Society for Consulting Psychology, and the Society of Psychologists in Management. Arthur received many honors over his long career, including the Harry and Miriam Levinson Award for Exceptional Contributions to Consulting Organizational Psychology awarded by the American Psychological Foundation of the American Psychological Association.

Beyond his considerable intellect and skills in organizational change and development, Arthur was a kind, generous, and principled human being with many friends and colleagues around the globe. He gave freely of his time and mentored a generation of consulting psychologists and organizational consultants. Arthur was also known for his wit and humorous stories (with appropriate accents) to illustrate the points he was making. It is fitting that he died on May 5, Cinco de Mayo, given his important accomplishments for and close friendship with the people of Mexico.

He greatly enriched our lives personally and professionally over several decades of collaboration. We and the profession of psychology are significantly diminished by his death.

RECOGNITION FOR DR. RODNEY LOWMAN

The authors would also like to express both their appreciation for and recognition of Dr. Rodney Lowman, who has supported this project from its initial conceptualization through each step in the process to bring it to your hands to read. For decades, Dr. Lowman has worked tirelessly to improve the theoretical and practical foundations for consulting psychology through his leadership and energetic efforts in editing our journals and in creating this book series for the Society of Consulting Psychology (Division 13 of the American Psychological Association). Every current and future general applied psychologist does and will owe him a debt of gratitude for a lifetime of service to all of us.

Essential Strategies for Organizational and Systems Change

1

Philosophical and Historical Foundation of Organizational and Systems Change

The scope of this book is broad. It covers human organizations and systems that (a) are small, medium, and large; (b) exist to make a profit; or (c) serve segments of society or the needs of local, national, and international governance. While social and societal, cultural, and national change has been the objective of kings, queens, military leaders, and religious leaders from time immemorial, the intellectual and scientific study of organizational and systems change (O/SC) has only emerged in more recent times. Even in the field of behavioral science and psychology, the study of strategies for O/SC is typically begun after mastery of more fundamental disciplines. In the field of psychology, for instance, it is assumed that graduates understand the processes covered in experimental psychology, learning theory, developmental psychology, psychopathology and treatment, social and organizational psychology, among other fields,

https://doi.org/10.1037/0000328-001
Essential Strategies for Organizational and Systems Change: An Overview for Consultants, by H. S. Leonard, R. R. Kilburg, and A. M. Freedman

before taking on the challenges of attempting to change organizations and complex social systems.

One unfortunate consequence of professional specialization is that students are introduced to an increasingly narrow spectrum of options for practice. Behavioral psychologists have expertise in shaping behavior using reward–nonreward and punishment strategies, but they may have a very limited understanding (or interest) in the impact of personality or covert processes on organizational/systems behavior. In a similar fashion, educators may have expert knowledge of developmental psychology and skill in using behavioral-shaping techniques but may feel overwhelmed by the political issues and organizational dynamics involved in attempting to bring about changes in educational practice in a large educational system. Clinical psychologists may have great success in helping their patients or clients function more productively at work and in their personal relationships but may feel that they have a limited understanding of how to change large-scale organizational and social systems.

In our experience, it is common practice for skilled professionals to apply a variation of the skills that they learned in their initial training and professional practices when trying to bring about changes in organizational or social systems. Therefore, it is typical for clinical and counseling psychologists to conceive of organizational problems in terms of psychopathology and, conversely, for organizational psychologists to overlook, downplay, or ignore the impact of psychopathology within organizations.

THE AUTHORS' APPROACH TO PREPARING CONSULTANTS TO CHANGE ORGANIZATIONS AND SYSTEMS

This book is written for students and professionals who have already achieved proficiency in one or more of the many specialties in the behavioral and psychological sciences and seek a more comprehensive understanding of change within organizations and human systems. Readers should not expect a simple treatment providing the ABCs of consultation to organizations and systems. O/SC is far too complex and even subtle to allow for such a linear and straightforward analysis. Our discussions will instead be more at the strategic rather than the tactical level. Further, our ambition is to provide a broad variety of "lenses" from which to view organizational problems and issues. Our hope is that this broadening experience will help organizational consultants of all persuasions (psychologists or otherwise) be more creative and effective in bringing about O/SC. Toward that end, this book provides a variety of practical "mental models" that consultants can use to frame and understand the problem as well as to craft interventions and promote their services with clients.

Because the goal of this book is to provide a concise description of several change strategies, we do not provide a comprehensive treatment of any one approach or strategy to O/SC. This is not another organization development or change management text. Rather, the book provides references and suggestions so that readers can follow up on their interest in any of the approaches and theories discussed. It should also be noted that while the strategies included in this book may be interventions at the individual, team, or organizational level, the criteria for success in all cases will focus on systems change, not on individual or team development. The literature and practice options for individual and team change are much too large to be covered in a concise treatment of O/SC.

HISTORICAL FOUNDATIONS FOR THE SCIENCE AND PRACTICE OF O/SC

One serious limitation of most previous treatments of OS/C is that they have been presented primarily from a Western philosophical position—more specifically, from a North American perspective.[1] This is understandable because the great bulk of the research has been done within Western academic communities. The next section of this book attempts to provide a more balanced view of change, incorporating key philosophical traditions and tenets that have influenced thought in action over several

[1] The text for this section of the chapter is from "The History and Current Status of Organizational and Systems Change," by H. S. Leonard, in H. S. Leonard, R. Lewis, A. M. Freedman, and J. Passmore (Eds.), *The Wiley-Blackwell Handbook of the Psychology of Leadership, Change, and Organizational Development* (pp. 239–266), 2013, Wiley-Blackwell UK (https://doi.org/10.1002/9781118326404.ch12). Copyright 2013 by Wiley-Blackwell UK. Reprinted with permission.

millennia. In addition, key philosophical as well as scientific controversies and debates that have influenced the practice of O/SC in recent decades are discussed.

Western and Eastern Approaches to Change

The matter of the impact and process of change has been on the minds of humans from the dawn of civilization. It is thought that the origins of the *I Ching*, the classic Book of Changes of the ancient Chinese civilization, were in existence as early as 1150 BCE (Blofeld, 1968) and were used by fortune-tellers and oracles. The philosophical treatment of change using the *I Ching* is generally attributed to Confucius and his followers and disciples beginning around 500 BCE (Wilhelm, 1960). The *I Ching*/Confucian philosophical position on change is that it is constant: "Change: that is the unchangeable" (Wilhelm, 1960, p. 23). In the *I Ching*/Confucian view, change and stability are of one; they are "neither kernel nor husk—heart and mind function together undivided" (Wilhelm, 1960, p. 13). This understanding is expressed in the three definitions of "I" in the *I Ching*; the "easy, the changing, and the constant" (Wilhelm, 1960, p. 15).

At about the same time in the Mediterranean, Heraclitus of Ephesus made parallel statements about the nature of change and stasis, holding that "life was movement that developed through the conflict of opposites" (Wilhelm, 1960, p. 13). In Heraclitus' view, nothing is permanent except change.

Despite the apparent similarities between the Chinese and Greek cultural viewpoints, there are important and characteristic differences. The *I Ching*/Confucian approach sees a complementarity and harmony between change and stability (Wilhelm, 1960). There is a unity to the two principles; in effect, they are two sides of the same coin. For Heraclitus, in contrast, a higher order of lawfulness, the Logos, promotes and shapes change (Wilhelm, 1960), creating coherency out of chaos. The unity and contrast among permanence, ubiquity, and stasis appear repeatedly in the various approaches to understanding change that are reviewed in this book. Each theory presented can be evaluated by the degree to which these models incorporate, integrate, and grapple with these eternal truths.

Distinctions, Debates, and Controversies

A number of ongoing distinctions, debates, and controversies are apparent in the literature regarding organizational change. They often take the form of polar positions and sometimes contradictory evidence advanced by researchers and theorists. In some cases, the dialectical debate has resulted in a useful synthesis of antithetical positions. For example, a number of researchers working in the post–World War II era viewed systems as largely controlled by inertial forces resulting in organizational processes demonstrating homeostasis and equilibrium (Hannan & Freeman, 1984; Katz & Kahn, 1978). Others, viewing organizational change through the lens of the economically disruptive 1970s, '80s, and '90s, viewed organizations as existing in an environment of continuous "whitewater"[2] with decreasing periods of calm and stability (Vaill, 1996). From this debate emerged a synthesis of these positions, punctuated equilibrium (Tushman & Romanelli, 1985). In this model, organizations may experience extended periods of relative calm and equilibrium where an evolutionary, convergent approach to change works well. However, the rapid incorporation of technology and advancement of knowledge makes punctuated, divergent, and radical change inevitable and therefore necessary.

The next sections provide an overview of various issues that continue to shape and influence the thinking of scholars, researchers, and practitioners.

Whether Object or Agent of Change

Change is a vastly different experience depending upon whether one is reacting to change (i.e., is the object of change) or is trying to bring about change (i.e., is the agent of change). If one is the object of change, it is easy to conclude, as did Heraclitus (Wheelwright, 1959), that change is constant, ubiquitous, and inexorable. From this perspective, it is also easy to see why many people in an organization will, at least initially, resist change. If one takes the perspective of a person who is being asked to change, it

[2]This term refers to the appearance of turbulent and frothy water flowing over shallow rapids in rivers.

makes sense to take a much more cautious and evolutionary approach that carefully involves all major stakeholders and end-users in the planning and implementation of the change (Cummings & Worley, 2015; McLean, 2005).

If, however, you are the agent of change, the process may appear more daunting. Most leaders and managers can attest to the difficulty bringing about significant and necessary change in complex organizations. Several sources have documented the rather low success rate (25%–33%) for organizational change interventions (Davenport, 1995; Pasmore, 2011; Schaffer & Thomson, 1992; Spector & Beer, 1994).

The difficulty that agents of change have in bringing about transformational or divergent (from the current strategies, practices, policies, etc.) change is explained by Hannan and Freeman (1984) as the result of the natural inertial and conservative characteristics of organizations and social systems. Natural selection in the marketplace "favors forms of organizations with high reliability of performance and high levels of accountability" (p. 154). Only large and significant internal or external stressors or crises are capable of overcoming the micro-adaptive and protective instincts that guide the decisions of leaders and managers.

Furthermore, Hannan and Freeman (1984) noted that the process of large strategic and structural organizational change makes transformational action unstable. The longer this process takes, the greater the risk of failure. Moreover, the fundamental changes wrought in transformational change mean that, in effect, the organization is being reborn and is subject to all the risks inherent in the start-up of a new organization.

It is no wonder that organizational resistance to inevitably disruptive transformational change is often seen at the middle-management and individual-contributor levels of the organization that are or will be the objects of the change effort. Senior leadership, in contrast, recognizing and having experienced numerous failed efforts to make transformational change, often discard their normal cautious and conservative leadership approaches to seize the opportunity afforded by crisis and threats to propose rapid, large, strategic, and structural changes in the organization. Rahm Emanuel, President Barack Obama's chief of staff, cited this principle in promoting the ambitious agenda included in the American Recovery and Reinvestment Act of 2009 when he stated, "Never let a serious crisis go to waste. What I mean by that is it's an opportunity to do things you couldn't do before" (Emanuel, 2009, p. 14).

Gersick (1991) proposed a cognitive model that describes the process of change during periods of crisis/threat-driven change. Following a period of confusion and questioning, leaders and managers synthesize a new vision. Referring to the paradigmatic change discussed by T. S. Kuhn (1996), Gersick noted that in larger systems, "the new direction does not emerge all at once; instead, a catalytic change opens the door to it" (p. 29).

ADAPTATION VERSUS SELECTION—DO ORGANIZATIONS REALLY CHANGE?

A related debate among change theorists is whether organizations really have the capacity to change (Demers, 2007). The issue is not whether organizations change because we have ample evidence that they do. The real issue is whether organizations have the capacity to recognize the need to change, develop a rational plan to accomplish this change, and have the political and implementation skills necessary to make change happen. This capacity has been termed *voluntary change* (Demers, 2007). A related issue is whether organizations can accomplish these changes rapidly enough that the transformations are completed before another crisis or threat requiring change emerges.

The relatively stable economic and political period after World War II and the optimism inspired by the victory over totalitarian forces led most scholars, researchers, and practitioners to assume that change could be brought about through rational and well-planned processes (Bennis et al., 1969; Golembiewski, 1972). During this period, change was equated with expansion, which seemed a normal and natural process (Demers, 2007). This assumption supported the belief that change is gradual, progressive, and emergent (Demers, 2007; Starbuck, 1971).

During this period, one group of theorists espoused the view that organizations could be purposeful and strategic in initiating change

(Child, 1997; Oliver, 1991; Sherer & Lee, 2002). They could—proactively, deliberately, and gradually—change the organization to achieve a strategic fit by choosing or influencing the environment (Demers, 2007).

A second group of scholars perceived a more reactive and reflective response, still rational, to crises, threats, and pressures perceived in their economic environment (Burns & Stalker, 1961; Lawrence & Lorsch, 1969; Thompson, 1967). In this approach, the change initiated would be contingent upon several factors (e.g., economic environment, technologies involved, size; Demers, 2007). The process of change in this view is seen as a "reactive, deliberate, piecemeal, gradual changes of strategy and/or structure to achieve functional equilibrium in reaction to change in contingencies" (Demers, 2007, p. 7).

Nevertheless, the dominant change model during this era was Lewin's (1947) notion of planned change through unfreezing, changing, and refreezing, combined with variants of general systems theory (GST; Katz & Kahn, 1978; von Bertalanffy, 1950) and sociotechnical systems (Emery & Trist, 1965). These models remain the core theoretical frameworks for a large majority of organization development (OD) practitioners and theorists to this day (see Cummings & Worley, 2015).

These change models also generally assume, following GST, that the normal state for organizational systems is a dynamic equilibrium with forces for change being balanced by forces resisting a change in performance level. This assumption is the basis for the well-known force field analysis methodology (Lewin, 1943). Lewin (1947) made it clear that the equilibrium level for an organizational system wasn't set at a certain level but could be moved through effective intervention.

The optimism of this period came to a close with the disruptions of the oil embargo in 1973 and the economic downturn and stagnation of the 1970s and early 1980s (Demers, 2007). These events ushered in a pessimistic period with theorists and practitioners wondering whether organizations had the capacity for voluntarily change in appropriate ways and rapidly enough to revitalize themselves and ensure survival. A number of scholars, based upon the experience of this later period, concluded that radical, nonincremental, and divergent changes to current strategy and structure change are rare because of inertia that is internal to the organization. Schumpeter's (1942/1975) concept of creative destruction (i.e., that destroying long-standing arrangements, assumptions, and institutions is necessary to free up the resources and energy required for innovation) came into vogue once again. Furthermore, radical and divergent change renders the organization vulnerable to several new, unexpected, or poorly understood factors and increases the probability that the organization will fail to survive (Demers, 2007). Viewing organizations as cautious, conservative systems with preferences for convergent thinking, these authors believed that only the shock of a life-threatening event could overcome an organization's inertia to produce the rapid, frame-shifting changes necessary for survival (Hannan & Freeman, 1984).

In keeping with this model of change, Hannan and Freeman (1984) described change as "the creation of new organizations and the demise of old ones" (p. 12). Also implied by this view is that organizational change follows the Darwinian model of evolution: Environmental failure leads to extinction with newer, more innovative generations of organisms/organizations taking over. Change, therefore, is an intergenerational process in which only new organizations acquire new traits, rather than a Lamarckian view wherein new traits can be learned within a generation (Van de Ven & Poole, 1995).

Top-Down Versus Bottom-Up Change

Change initiated by decisions made by top leadership is commonly thought of as "top down" (Demers, 2007). In contrast, change that begins with grassroots involvement and decisions that "bubble up" to top leadership is commonly thought of as "bottom up" (Demers, 2007). Those who believe that planned change is possible, if not preferable, tend to make decisions about strategic goals and develop an implementation plan that is pushed down through the organization. This decision style has been described as *strategic choice* by Child (1997). In practice, this approach is often termed *strategic management* (Hamel et al., 1999).

While most strategic management practitioners would, undoubtedly, recommend close consultation and collaboration with key stakeholders and constituents in developing implementation plans and managing the change process (Freeman, 1984), nevertheless, the strategic goals and top-level strategy would be developed by top leadership. This consultation should occur, if for no other reason, to prevent stakeholder groups from organizing through political action to resist the planned change (Demers, 2007; Quinn, 1980).

Although there is less literature that systematically discusses bottom-up change (Demers, 2007), the *action research* variant of OD (Freedman, 2006) provides a methodology for surfacing the views of various stakeholder groups from top management to end-users to provide implementation plans that benefit both from insights across hierarchies and functional units as well as less political action that may impede the eventual implementation process (French & Bell, 1973). The action research approach is closely linked to Lewin's (1951) unfreezing–changing–refreezing model, whereby organizations desiring to bring about change first conduct extensive data collection and feedback activities with all organizational groups and stakeholders who will be affected by, or have interests in, the changes or goals to be achieved. The change agents then work with the client organization to develop the resulting implementation plan.

Political action, however, is not always seen as a negative factor in organizational change. Kanter (1983), in studying change in 10 large corporations, noted the positive role of politics in successful bottom-up change efforts. In her analysis, large "macro-change" often occurred after the accumulation of many "micro-changes" that were promoted by individuals or stakeholder groups. She observed that there was a direct correlation between the power given to individuals and stakeholders groups and the ability of the organization to avoid stagnation through continuous innovation.

Action Learning, not to be confused with action research, also makes implicit assumptions about the importance of grassroots knowledge and interests in developing superior solutions to complex and vexing problems. Marquardt et al. (2009) required that Action Learning teams have sufficient diversity in status, knowledge, and perspective to ensure not only that the problem analysis includes a broadly shared understanding of and agreement on what the root problem is and what contributes to that problem but also includes their formal and tacit knowledge when formulating an implementation plan.

Methodology of Inquiry: Dynamic Versus Descriptive

A distinction can be made between models that are based on efforts to change organizations versus those that describe how organizations have already changed. The former perspective can be described as a dynamic one in which a practical theory of change is developed by taking action, reflecting on the result, drawing conclusions about what promoted or interfered with change, and adjusting the theory accordingly. This learning paradigm was popularized by Kolb (1984) and executed in Action Learning (Marquardt et al., 2009; Revans, 1983). Lewin is rightfully revered as a social psychologist because of his insistence that theory is of practical as well as intellectual value: "nothing is as practical as a good theory" (Lewin in Marrow, 1969, p. 169). Lewin also noted that the best way to learn about an organization or system is to try to change it (Marrow, 1969). This is the change model that forms the dynamic basis for specific change strategies such as Action Learning (Marquardt et al., 2009).

Four Lenses on Change

Van de Ven and Poole (1995) described four basic models (or, in their terms, engines) of change that integrate much of the thinking described in the organizational change literature.

Teleological

Perhaps the most popular model, because it aligns so well with typical OD practice models, the teleological model includes a cycle of goal formulation, implementation, evaluation, and modification of action or goals based on what is learned or desired by the organization or social system. This model aligns well with Lewinian thinking as articulated by theorists such as Kolb (1984). This model focuses on purposeful enactment, social construction, and consensus, all familiar and comfortable operational concepts for mainstream OD and change management theorists and practitioners.

Life Cycle

This model is also quite popular in OD and change management literature. It describes the process of organization change in terms of stages of development from "birth" to "death" or demise of an organization. These stages frequently describe a cycle including (a) start-up, (b) growth, (c) harvest or maturity, (d) decline, (e) life crisis, and (f) renewal or death. These models focus on the forecasting of growth and decline, appropriate regulation of growth and development, and compliant adaptation. This model borrows heavily from the frameworks developed in GST (Katz & Kahn, 1978; von Bertalanffy, 1969).

Evolution

Evolutionary models describe a repetitive sequence based on a Darwinian framework of natural variation, selection of the most able or fit, and retention of these characteristics in future generations (Darwin, 1859). The popular "best practices" approach to organizational decision-making follows this model. Competition for scarce resources drives this process.

Dialectic

This model borrows from a Hegelian model of change wherein conflicts developing between organizations and social systems produce a synthesis and an accepted model that is later confronted by newer approaches and ideas (Benson, 1977). Confrontation and conflict provide the energy for inevitable change and progress (measured in terms of survival). Schumpeter's (1942/1975) model of creative destruction has much in common with this model.

ORGANIZATIONAL AND SYSTEMS CHANGE STRATEGIES PRESENTED IN THIS BOOK

A diverse group of strategies are offered in this book that can be applied to achieve organizational and systems change. Some, like OD, psychodynamic theory, and learning strategies, can be used directly to achieve

O/SC. Other strategies such an organizational systems theory are used more indirectly to understand organizations, plan change strategies, and manage the organizational change process. Following is a brief summary for each of the O/SC strategies presented in this book.

Chapter 2. Organizations as Systems

This chapter provides several systems models used in O/SC, including general systems theory (von Bertalanffy, 1950), Alfred Kuhn's (1972) logic of social systems, Senge's (1990) system thinking, and relevant theory and research from family systems theories (Bateson, 1972; Haley, 1976; Palazzoli, 1978; Watzlawick et al., 1974).

Chapter 3. Lewinian, Organization Development, and Change Management

This chapter integrates Lewinian social psychology with the emerging field of O/SC. This chapter introduces the core theory and science that was incorporated into early OD strategies. It also covers OD, change management, and consulting in a VUCA (vulnerable, uncertain, complex, and ambiguous) world as well as in organizational systems in chaotic and dynamically unstable environments.

Chapter 4. Leading and Managing Radical Change

This chapter extends the earlier Lewinian strategies to situations requiring radical change. It also provides a phenomenological view of the process of change—what it feels like to lead or be the object of change as well as key stages in organizational reaction and evolution.

Chapter 5. Covert Processes in Human Affairs

This chapter describes how an understanding of psychodynamics and covert processes within organizations can be leveraged to achieve O/SC.

Chapter 6. Learning-Based Change

This chapter describes and traces the learning-based strategies first developed in laboratory education in the 20th century in the United States and continuing and merging with other action-based strategies such as Action Learning into the 21st century.

Chapter 7. Positive Psychology, Behaviorism, and Neuropsychology and the Future of Organizational and Systems Change

This chapter describes some important contributors to the art and science of O/SC, such as positive psychology, behaviorism, and neuropsychology as well as predictions for the future of O/SC.

In conclusion, this book provides the reader with an understanding of the theoretical and conceptual foundations of O/SC as well as descriptions of the most popular and commonly used O/SC strategies.

2

Organizations as Systems

The concept of organizational systems was relatively novel before the introduction of general systems theory (GST) by von Bertalanffy and colleagues in the mid-20th century. Before that time, organizations were described as linear and hierarchical bureaucracies (Weber, 1921/2021) and as controlled through a variety of interrelated management functions (Fayol, 1949). The theories in this chapter describe organizations as composed of and residing within holistic systems of processes and events and marked a dramatic break from the mechanistic, static, and rule-bound approach to management that tended to treat employees as interchangeable gears in the economic enterprise (Taylor, 2011).

Looking at organizations as systems is a new way of looking at organizational behavior. Instead of looking at organizations as interlocking grids of authority, responsibilities, and contingencies for compliance, the systemic approaches presented in this chapter pertain to what is known in

https://doi.org/10.1037/0000328-002
Essential Strategies for Organizational and Systems Change: An Overview for Consultants, by H. S. Leonard, R. R. Kilburg, and A. M. Freedman

fields as diverse as biology, physics, psychology, sociology, psychotherapy, and even cybernetics and that can be applied to the understanding of organizational behavior. In the post–World War II era, this was a relatively novel approach for organizational psychology.

GENERAL SYSTEMS THEORY AND CHANGE

GST was introduced by von Bertalanffy (1950) at about the same time that Lewin (1951) formulated his field theory. Starting in the 1930s, von Bertalanffy's efforts were designed initially to determine what structures and processes were held in common by all living creatures. The publication of his ideas post–World War II coincided with the rise of information theory and cybernetics, and they all quickly merged into a powerful set of concepts and tools for the exploration of patterns of organization in virtually every field of study.

Many of the basic tenets of field theory and GST are similar, and thus it is only natural that followers of Lewin would embrace GST and use the theoretical rigor of GST to undergird their research and theory. Two basic similarities between field theory and GST stand out. First, both theoretical perspectives are holistic and concerned with the relationships between the relevant elements of the psychological field or system rather than focusing on only one or two variables at a time. Both approaches view the dynamic relationships among elements or variables at a given time, rather than focusing on a linear chain of events in a small group of variables.

Just as Lewin had a multidisciplinary history, GST developed over several decades through a cross-disciplinary group of theorists that included von Bertalanffy (1950), a biologist; Boulding (1960), an economist; Ashby (1958), a bacteriologist; Miller (1955), a psychiatrist; Rapoport (1956), a mathematician; and Emery and Trist (1960) and Katz and Kahn (1978), organizational theorists and psychologists.

In common parlance among organizational and systems change (O/SC) consultants, GST is often referred to as *open systems theory*. Before the mid-20th century, most scientific theory assumed a conservation of energy within a system. That is, the amount of energy in any system, nonliving or living, was constant over time (Newton, 1687/1999). In the psychological theories of this time, including Freudian theory, "hydraulic" analogies were common. While these assumptions worked reasonably well when considering smaller, firmly bounded systems, many theorists, including von Bertalanffy, noted that larger systems, freely interacting and often nested within each other, demonstrated open and permeable boundaries or interfaces that did not operate strictly according to the orthodox laws of physics.

Organizations, from a GST perspective, are complicated places. They like stability but are constantly knocked off balance by unexpected or unknowable factors and events. There are great advantages to growth, diversification, and creation of monopolies where they do not need to compete so hard. These processes, however, bring their own problems of integration, coordination, and complacency, which undermine flexibility, creativity, or the desire to change. Organizational systems try to stay in balance with a long-term perspective, but they do so at the risk of being unprepared or unpracticed in dealing with shorter term turbulence. GST can be described as a model of organizational systems close to, but never quite in, equilibrium. GST can also be described as a linear (i.e., the effects of events are additive) systems model wherein most events and behaviors are predictable most, but not all, of the time.

GST does not provide a set of strategies for implementing organizational change. Instead, it provides a manual that explains how social and organizational systems work. GST presents the structural model that provides the insights necessary for organization development practitioners to develop initial plans for change that could be implemented and subsequently modified based on data gathered while monitoring the process (see the action research model in the next section). The common structure and characteristics of all open systems are presented in Figure 2.1 (following Ashby, 1958; Boulding, 1960; Miller, 1955; and von Bertalanffy, 1969).

IMPORTATION, TRANSFORMATION, AND EXPORTATION OF ENERGY

All open systems have input → throughput (energy transformation or "work") → output energy cycles. Systems have rich "feedback" links that help the system regulate the amount of input and output and the form of

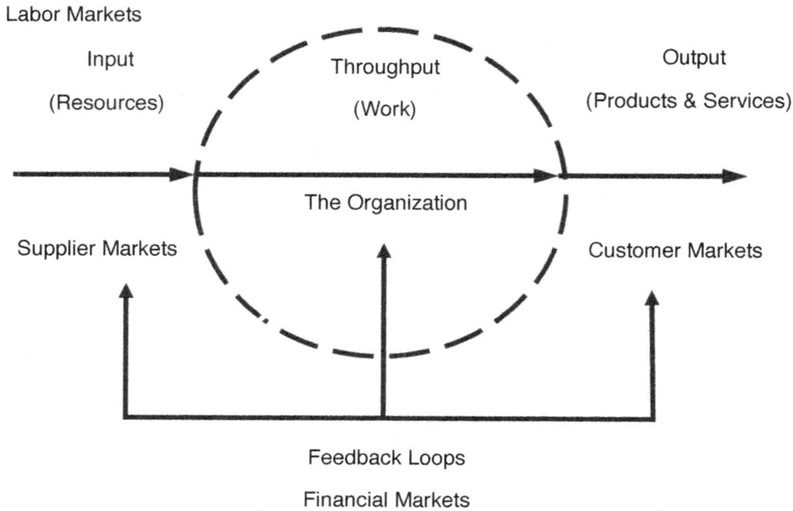

Figure 2.1

Note. Basic open systems framework for relating inputs, throughput, output, and feedback links for an organization.

the transformation process. This basic and familiar open systems framework is easy to relate to standard manufacturing processes and provides an accessible and understandable framework for both practitioners and organizational clients.

Systems as Cycles of Events

Typically, systems have a repetitive cycle of inputs → throughput → output (Katz & Kahn, 1978). Ford produces cars and trucks, Harvard produces graduates, and so on. The primary task of this cycle of events is to preserve and sustain the organization. Each system has a primary task that is critical for its survival. When an organizational system improperly identifies or ignores its primary task, it no longer finds customers for its output or products and runs the danger of becoming incapacitated or of even dying. These cycles of events constitute the structure of the system (Allport, 1962).

Negative Entropy

The universal law of entropy, also known as the second law of thermodynamics (Fermi, 1956), states that all systems move toward disorganization, decay, and death. This process is reversed (negative entropy) while the system is alive and sustaining itself. To ensure that systems stay alive and thrive, constant importation of energy or the ability to store energy is required to carry the system through lean energy periods.

Suprasystems and Subsystems

Every system is embedded in a larger system (the suprasystem) and is also composed of smaller systems (subsystems). We often refer to the system's suprasystem as its environment or ecosystem. Subsystems are component parts of a system that are separated by boundaries and are internally consistent regarding quantity, quality, frequency, or phase of energy utilization. In organizations, these subsystems may be termed departments, business units, or project teams, for example.

Positive and Negative Feedback

Feedback is useful information to manage or regulate the system. Positive feedback is a message to continue or even amplify current behavior. Negative feedback, on the other hand, is a message to diminish or even discontinue current behavior. Positive and negative feedback function very much like the thermostat in a house or a combustion engine.

The Steady State of Dynamic Equilibrium

The cycle of energy conversion in an organizational system operates best or most efficiently when there is a relatively stable dynamic state. In other words, systems trend toward dynamic equilibrium if undisturbed by unexpected turbulence. Therefore, organizations tend to resist changes in the energy dynamics and will only do so if accomplishment of the organization's primary task is threatened. This is one reason why periods of crisis represent such good opportunities for change.

Growth and Expansion

Although organizations prefer stability, they also need to grow to survive. One reason for the need to grow is instability in the energy supply; organizations learn that they must generate surpluses or resource reserves to buffer the organization in lean economic times. Growth can be accomplished through expansion of current production, through diversification of production, or by creating monopolies that capture the organization's supply and/or distribution chains. Each of these activities gives the organization more control over its environment and destiny.

Differentiation

Open systems develop through differentiation and elaboration. Start-up organizations have a very simple structure with organizational members carrying out multiple roles. As organizations grow, roles become more diversified, structured, and specialized, and additional subsystems (departments and business units) are created. This development allows for more efficiency, which gives the organization more survival capability. On the other hand, increased specialization diminishes the flexibility and adaptability of the organization.

Integration and Coordination

Growth, expansion, and differentiation place great demands on an organizational system to integrate and coordinate its component parts. In organizational systems, integration and coordination serve different purposes (Katz & Kahn, 1978). Integration ensures that organizational members share the same norms and values, while coordination ensures that differentiated tasks and roles mesh properly.

Equifinality

This principle states that a system can reach the same final state from differing initial conditions and by a variety of paths. Equifinality provides flexibility for the organizational system to be creative in inventing new, novel, and more effective ways to accomplish its primary task. This flexibility, however, is inhibited if its structure is too rigid or if it becomes overencumbered with policy and procedures.

THE LOGIC OF SOCIAL SYSTEMS

By the 1960s and 1970s, systems-based change theories had broad impact and appeal in a broad spectrum of the social (A. Kuhn, 1972), organizational (Katz & Kahn, 1978), and administrative sciences (Hirschhorn, 1988). For instance, A. Kuhn (1972) and A. Kuhn and Beam (1982) made what remains one of the most consistent and illuminating applications of systems thinking to the study of organizations. Kuhn posited several essential types of organizational systems. *Acting systems* comprise elements relating to each other in such a way as to produce outcomes of various types. Acting systems are either controlled, meaning they have at least one goal that directs their effort and produces an equilibrium, or uncontrolled, in which case the elements interact and produce outcomes, but those are not goal driven and produce no specific state of equilibrium. *Pattern systems* are those with at least two elements that relate to each other within a criterion or set of criteria inside of action systems but do not themselves act.

Systems comprise detectors, selectors, and effectors that are organized either hierarchically into subsystems, systems, and suprasystems or into networks of various types. *Detectors* obtain and communicate information of various types. *Selectors* evaluate information and make choices. *Effectors* put decisions into action. As stated earlier, systems develop to achieve an equilibrium. They have emergent properties through which they can change significantly and rapidly in form, process, and content. They also have regressive properties in which they decay and can cease to exist in any form. Kuhn derived more than a thousand propositions concerning systems. These powerful concepts continue to influence most of the theory and practice of change management today (Cummings & Worley, 2015; Gharajedaghi, 2011).

These approaches to the study and management of organizations offer leaders and consultants a virtual cornucopia of ideas, methods, and models for creating, assessing, and changing enterprises. Most of the time, they provide either general or specific descriptions of the elements of systems, the ways in which they interact, the outcomes they produce, and, therefore, how they can be directed and modified. The essence of modern administrative approaches is to collect data on these systemic components of organizational operations that then enable leaders to engage rational choice making on a moment-to-moment or longer-term strategic basis.

A wide variety of change management and organization development interventions are commonly employed within the broad approaches suggested by open systems theory and what we could call Kuhn's concepts. If we look at Kuhn's delineation of detector, selector, and effector components of systems, the following methods are often seen:

- *detector changes*—marketing surveys and sales forecasts, competitor analyses, satisfaction surveys, engagement surveys, culture analyses, risk management assessments, strategic planning efforts, environmental scans, and needs analyses
- *selector changes*—strategy reviews, mission, vision and values assessments, culture changes, policy, practices, procedural and process reviews that change decision criteria, membership in leadership groups, and succession management
- *effector changes*—acquisitions and mergers designed to modify market positions, reorganizations to increase effectiveness and efficiencies, creation of task forces, work groups, crisis management teams in response to challenges and opportunities, communication methods or messaging changes, advertising and sales policy changes, product and service redesigns, public advocacy efforts, and lobbying

These lists are by no means exhaustive. Any careful examination of a consultation project will quickly uncover elements of systems concepts and considerations in operation. Virtually every change to an organizational chart requires a careful examination of structural and process considerations in an enterprise. Adding members to any work or leadership group to increase diversity and inclusion or to meet expertise objectives will also immediately require many adaptations to organizational processes. Such interventions also frequently create changes to the content of the communications and the types of information exchanged in, and by, a group. Modifying any manufacturing or service delivery process, by applying lean sigma methods, for instance, may well produce significant shifts in either the steps organizations use or in the outcomes anticipated.

SENGE AND SYSTEMS THINKING

Although Peter Senge (1990) is perhaps best known for promoting the value of learning within organizations (see Chapter 6), he also popularized the notion of *systems thinking*, which he identified as the fifth and most important discipline necessary for creating true learning organizations. Although Senge never mentioned or even cited GST, his description of the elements and dynamics of systems thinking clearly was influenced by the systems models first presented in the early 1950s (Boulding, 1960; Emery & Trist, 1960; Miller, 1955; von Bertalanffy, 1950, 1969).

> Systems thinking is a conceptual framework, a body of knowledge and tools that has been developed over the past 50 years, to make macro as well as micro patterns clearer, and to help us see how to change them effectively. (Senge, 1990, p. 7)

Senge offered these additional systems principles that are relevant to organizational learning and change.

TODAY'S PROBLEMS COME FROM YESTERDAY'S "SOLUTIONS"

This outcome is often the consequence of "fighting" the last war and applying a short-term, transactional solution to a problem requiring a long-term, comprehensive, and systems solution. Applying a short-term, non–systems-based, and transactional solution to a complex problem too often shifts problems from one part of the system to another part. Overreliance on "best practices" runs the danger of applying an obsolete or irrelevant solution to a situation that differs in significant ways from earlier circumstances.

The Harder You Push, the Harder the System Pushes Back[1]

This principle follows from Lewin's (1943) earlier mental model of the force-field analysis. Lewin reasoned that for a behavior to remain reasonably balanced or stable (he termed this a *quasi-stationary state*), there must be some form of dynamic equilibrium. Because systems prefer to stay in a condition of "steady state" or dynamic equilibrium as a consequence of the second law of thermodynamics (Fermi, 1956), elements of the organizational system that are being "pushed" can be expected to push back. The harder that an element of the organizational system is pushed, the harder it will push back.

Behavior Grows Better Before It Grows Worse

Many short-term solutions work initially but may lead to a much more serious problem later because collateral issues are not being addressed. This is a variation of the familiar "kicking the can down the road" analogy. In many cases, there is an awareness of the danger of addressing the symptom without treating the underlying cause, but there is also a hope (often irrational) that the problem will not reemerge later with larger consequences.

The Easy Way Out Usually Leads Back In

Using the tried and familiar solutions to problems has the virtues of being simple, efficient, and often the easiest approach. As long as the problem

[1] All the subtitles in this section (but not the text following each subtitle) are direct quotes from Senge, 1990, pp. 57–67.

being addressed is familiar and well understood, these simple solutions usually work well. That is the appeal of identifying "best practices" for common problems. Following well-tested procedures and protocols makes good sense in a high percentage of situations.

When a novel or unprecedented problem emerges, however, more difficult, time-consuming problem-solving processes that require a change in perspective and operating principles are required. Only through these processes can the organization correctly diagnose the real versus the presenting problem, establish appropriate goals, identify root causes and possible solutions, choose the best solutions, and execute the appropriate remedies. This approach takes a lot more time, energy, and commitment than applying a formulaic "best practice."

The Cure Can Be Worse Than the Disease

Most solution attempts are well intended. However, in many situations, the law of unintended consequences kicks in. Examples abound to illustrate this dynamic. Rationing to ensure order and fairness in a marketplace with scarcities often incites panic buying and hoarding. Rent control creates disincentives for building more housing. Increasing government assistance for basic services frequently increases dependence on government, thus creating another, more intractable problem. If the more fundamental problems are not addressed, we only succeed in shifting the burden from one part of the system to another.

Faster Is Slower

In systems, there is often an optimal rate for change or growth. Going too fast without addressing the natural and normal resistance to change risks can, paradoxically, slow things down and sow the seeds for ultimate failure. When dealing with pandemics (as we are while we write this book), for example, prematurely suspending social distancing and other epidemic mitigation measures raises the risk of a new wave of infections and a delay in a sustained return to normal life.

Cause and Effect Are Not Closely Related in Time and Space

It is very common to treat immediate symptoms rather than the underlying and often long-term cause. So, if sales are lagging, organizations first look for solutions within the sales function when, in fact, the real problem may have been caused by other, more distant, factors, such as poor design, changes in consumer tastes, or production problems. Also, the consequences of actions we take today may not be seen or felt for many years. The trend toward evaluating and paying CEOs according to their impact on shareholder value (stock prices) began in the 1980s. Decades later, the consequences of these actions were observed. Corporations used profits to buy back their company's stock, thereby raising stock value beyond its intrinsic value and raising salaries for CEOs and senior executives (Useem, 2019). This practice resulted in greatly elevated CEO/senior executive salaries compared with pay for their employees and significantly expanded wealth inequalities.

Small Changes Can Produce Big Results—But the Areas of Highest Leverage Are Often the Least Obvious

Equal effort does not necessarily result in equal effects. In some places and situations, the "leverage" is much more favorable for change. So, for example, every organization has "pivotal" roles—roles wherein competence and talent have more impact than in other roles. Many would assume that these roles would reside in senior leadership. These positions are certainly important, but competing for the best executive talent can be very expensive. Points of maximum leverage, however, have a big payoff relative to the investment—that is, they have high leverage value.

Consider, for example, the relative payoff for two roles at Disney theme parks—individuals playing Mickey Mouse and the street cleaners and general grounds maintenance personnel. It can be argued (Boudreau & Ramstad, 2007) that the street cleaners have a larger, and nonobvious, impact on the success of the Disney theme parks than the Mickey Mouse role players. The explanation is counterintuitive. Because the role of Mickey Mouse is so scripted and controlled, the relative cost of hiring and training people for this role is fairly low—that is, you don't need to pay a lot more to get a good versus poor performer for this role. However, the overall experience at Disney World is highly dependent on customer service. When you need assistance as a customer, who do you approach? Mickey Mouse? The role-playing Mickey Mouse never speaks—that would be out of role. Customers usually seek out one of the ground crew and maintenance members. The selection and training of grounds and maintenance people make a big difference. A little more pay and better selection processes make a big difference in the customer experience. The leverage involved in investment in this role, therefore, is much higher than with the Mickey Mouse role players.

You Can Have Your Cake and Eat It Too—But Not at Once

Many problems in organizations present themselves as dilemmas that can't be rationally solved. For instance, the demands of customers to have products that are of higher quality, cheaper, and developed more quickly would appear to be a dilemma. The organization can provide for only two of these three demands simultaneously. Senge (1990) argued that focusing on one or two customer desires would ultimately, but not immediately, improve the third factor. For instance, improvement in cycle-time for product development frequently, over time, produces lower production costs and higher quality. Many of what are apparently "either–or choices" disappear using a larger systems perspective matched with intelligent sequencing of priorities.

Dividing an Elephant in Half Does Not Produce Two Small Elephants

You cannot understand an organization or any system by focusing on or studying only one element. The familiar "blind men and the elephant" story illustrates this principle. If you are blind and only grab hold of the elephant's trunk, you might think the elephant is like a tree. If you grab the elephant's ear, on the other hand, you might be convinced that an elephant is like a large, broad rug. Managers and employees are bound to see their organization differently depending on the functional "silo" they work in. An organization can only be understood and appreciated by looking across organizational boundaries. One way to do this is to establish strong relationships across organizational units. Organizations can enhance system knowledge by rotating managers through a variety of functions—line and staff—as individuals progress up the managerial or leadership ladder.

There Is No Blame

It is natural to make "us versus them" distinctions. At the time of publication of Senge's book in 1990, it was common to pick winners and losers, to assign blame for failures, and to punish managers and organizational units for organizational failures. This pattern of "kicking butt and taking names" following failures and errors was identified as a reason for the lack of initiative and willingness to take well-calculated risks, problems that held back economic growth and business success.

With the rise of start-up cultures characteristic of Silicon Valley and technology firms, however, the stigma of failure and the resulting blame have been greatly reduced. This change has given rise to slogans such as "fail fast and learn faster." Nevertheless, the tendency to assign blame, personal and organizational, is still common and inevitably increases resistance to taking smart risks and showing initiative. This pattern breaks down healthy connective tissue between individuals and organizational units.

BATESON, WATZLAWICK, AND THE PALO ALTO GROUP—INTERPERSONAL AND FAMILY SYSTEMS[2]

Systems-based theories and concepts developed in clinical fields such as family therapy (Bowen, 1976; Haley, 1976; Minuchin, 1974; Palazzoli, 1978; Watzlawick et al., 1974) and community mental health (Dalton et al., 2001) can also be usefully applied to organizational change efforts.

[2] Some of the text for this section is from "The History and Current Status of Organizational and Systems Change," by H. S. Leonard, in H. S. Leonard, R. Lewis, A. M. Freedman, and J. Passmore (Eds.), *The Wiley-Blackwell Handbook of the Psychology of Leadership, Change, and Organizational Development* (pp. 252–256), 2013, Wiley-Blackwell UK (https://doi.org/10.1002/9781118326404.ch12). Copyright 2013 by Wiley-Blackwell UK. Reprinted with permission.

Levels of Change

The impact of Gregory Bateson on intra- and interpersonal change cannot be overstated. Trained as an anthropologist, Bateson already had a substantial international reputation as a thought leader in the emerging and developing fields of linguistics, systems theory, and cybernetics when he joined a small multidisciplinary group at the Mental Research Institute (MRI) in Palo Alto studying the impact of interpersonal and systems factors on mental illness.

Gregory Bateson and his colleagues (Don Jackson, a psychiatrist; Jay Haley, a family therapist; and John Weakland, an anthropologist) developed the well-known double-bind theory for the maintenance, if not genesis, of schizophrenia (Bateson et al., 1956). In essence, Bateson and his colleagues hypothesized that peculiar or crazy behavior of the person with schizophrenia can be explained by the existence of contradictory and paradoxical messages of the form, "Do A or I'll punish you" while at the same time also communicating, "If you do A, you will get punished just the same." Since the individual cannot do either without incurring punishment, he or she behaves in a new and novel way to escape the double-bind.

Several of Bateson's colleagues at MRI (Watzlawick et al., 1974) supported this theory in an ingenious way by referring to two 19th-century mathematical theories (Bateson, 1972). Using the theory of groups, these authors noted that a group comprised a collection of members that have at least one common characteristic and whose combination of two or more members of the group is also part of the group. Take, for instance, the traditional method for telling time (i.e., 24 hours in the day). If you add 4 hours to 11 p.m., the time would be 3 a.m., a number which is part of the group. Furthermore, one may combine members of their group in any order and get the same result. Groups also contain an identity member that, when combined with other members of the group, returns to the original member. For instance, in groups whose rule of combination is additive, the identity member is 0 (e.g., $7 + 0 = 7$). Finally, every group member has a reciprocal or opposite so that the combination of any member with its opposite yields the identity member (e.g., 0). Using the rule of combination, 7 plus its opposite (−7) yields 0, the identity member.

First-Order Change

Watzlawick et al. (1974) used these principles to explain what the authors describe as *first-order change*, transformations in which the results closely resemble one of the members of the group. For example, applying a standard, familiar approach to a problem, you are likely to get a familiar solution, one that may or may not solve the problem. If nothing is done to solve the problem, nothing happens (the identity of the member is retained). Again, this outcome may or may not be beneficial to the problem owner. Finally, trying to do the opposite of what is currently happening will frequently lead to no change at all because the two behaviors cancel themselves out.

These principles can also be applied to organizational change: It often requires a jump in the conceptual level of a problem to achieve real change. Kuhn (Thomas, not Alfred; 1962/1996) referred to this as a *paradigm shift*.

Understanding Problem Persistence and the Need for Second-Order Change

Why is it, one may ask, that people, teams, and organizations continue to apply the same solutions and get the same results? Most readers will be familiar with the following quote: "Insanity is doing the same thing over and over again and expecting different results" (attributed to Einstein). The identity of a new "solution" that does not solve the original problem is referenced in the French proverb *Plus ça change, plus c'est la meme chose*—"the more things change, the more they stay the same."

Watzlawick et al. (1974) reasoned that people in families, social systems, and organizations are trying to affect change but are using first-order change strategies that almost guarantee the problem will not be solved or that a new but familiar result will emerge that is as problematic as the presenting problem. The familiar oscillation between efforts to centralize and decentralize operations in an organization is an example of a system caught in a first-order change behavioral circle. Overreliance on "best practices" also ensures that organizations will be using good solutions that have worked in the past in situations with some similarities but may not be appropriate for a new, unforeseen, and therefore disruptive situation.

First-order change solutions are usually based on conventional, commonsense past experience. If these solutions have been successful in the past and the presenting situation is sufficiently familiar or similar to past situations encountered by the organization, these solutions have a reasonable chance of success. The rub comes when new and unprecedented problems confront the organization for which no current acceptable solution exists (i.e., the appropriate solution is not part of the current set of solutions). In this situation, transformational, or second-order, change strategies that transcend a given system or frame of reference are required.

This jump to a higher, or at least unique, level of conceptualization is what, as noted earlier, Kuhn (1962/1996) described as a paradigm shift. To address new and unprecedented situations and problems, managers and leaders are constantly being encouraged to "think outside the box."

Strategies for Achieving Second-Order Change

Bateson (1972) and Watzlawick et al. (1974) agreed with Confucius that change and persistence cannot be considered in isolation; one needs to understand persistence to comprehend, much less bring about, change. This realization will lead the successful change agent to examine why people (a) ignore the need to change; (b) are fearful of change; (c) keep applying failed solutions; and (d) vastly oversimplify the situation, the factors involved in a problem, and the necessary actions to solve a problem.

It is difficult—and, in many cases, impossible—to provide instructions for directly solving a problem requiring a second-order solution. After all, in most cases, conventional and commonsense solutions have already been tried and failed. Furthermore, Watzlawick et al. (1974) reported that even effective second-order change agents frequently cannot easily identify what they did that brought about change. These change agents, however, employed various strategies that set the stage for change and had great confidence that individuals and systems would make corrections or find solutions to problems, unconsciously if not consciously, to get out of the unconstructive, destructive, and self-defeating "doom-loops" in which they found themselves.

Following is a sample of some second-order change tactics proposed by Watzlawick et al. (1974).

Frustrate the Change

One second-order change tactic is to openly predict that the individual or client system cannot change; that they are powerless to change given all the obstacles and impediments that they face. This strategy works on two principles: (a) People respond well to challenges, especially if others underestimate them; and (b) reverse psychology—people often reflexively react to instruction by moving in the opposite or a new direction.

Show Appreciation for the Efforts of Individuals and Members Who Are Doing What They Think Is Best for the Client System

This strategy reflects the belief that individuals in the system are trying their best to make good decisions and believe they are taking appropriate action for the welfare and survival of the system. This principle is consistent with the appreciative inquiry strategy (Cooperrider, 1999) and the positive psychology approach (Snyder & Lopez, 2001) of focusing on strengths and positive aspirations rather than deficiencies and dysfunctional behavior. In many cases, showing appreciation and respect for efforts that the client system is making to solve a problem minimizes defensiveness and allows the client system to explore other solutions that hold more promise. When debriefing problem-solving efforts, it is usually more effective to ask a team to reflect on what they did well rather than how they failed or what they did poorly. With these efforts recognized and appreciated, the team can then be asked for areas where it can improve even more (Marquardt et al., 2009).

Ask More Questions About *What* Solutions Have Been Tried Rather Than Trying to Figure Out *Why* the Situation Is Difficult to Change

In many cases, the solution that is attempted is the problem. If one can suppress the urge to ask why something is happening and focus more on what the system is trying to do to correct the problem, the resulting investigation will provide information about why the problem is persisting and how first-order change efforts may actually be perpetuating and supporting the associated problem. With this information, one may be able to formulate a second-order plan that has promise as a means of upsetting dysfunctional patterns of interaction.

Reframe the Situation

Reframing changes the "conceptual and/or emotional setting or emotional setting or viewpoint in relation to which a situation is experienced" and places "it in another frame which fits the 'facts' of the same concrete situation equally well or even better, and thereby changes its entire meaning" (Watzlawick et al., 1974, p. 93). During one of the many 19th-century riots in Paris, the commander of an army detachment was ordered to clear a city square by firing into the *canaille* (disorderly rabble). Instead, the commander ordered his troops to level their rifles at the crowd and commenced to bellow at the top of his lungs, "Mesdames, m'sieurs, I have orders to fire at the canaille. But as I see a great number of honest, respectable citizens before me, I request that they leave so that I can safely shoot the canaille" (Watzlawick et al., 1974, p. 81). The square emptied very quickly after this reframing of the situation by the commander. The facts on the ground had not changed nor had the commander's orders. By reframing the crowd as a mixture of law-abiding citizens and lawless rabble, however, the commander had altered the situation to both the advantage of the crowd as well as the long-term interests of the state.

Create Paradoxes That Make It Difficult for the Client System to Persist in Its Current Dysfunctional Behavior

Creating paradoxes to change behavior is an advanced tactic and is typically attempted when all other efforts fail. Paradoxical tactics seem risky because they often prescribe the symptom to the client. Some paradoxical instructions seem harmless enough—for example, instructing a micromanaging executive to keep even tighter control over subordinates. Others may appear potentially counterproductive or even dangerous—such as confronting organizational leaders about the reasons they want the organization to change when it is still profitable.

SYSTEMS IN DISEQUILIBRIUM—CHAOS AND COMPLEXITY THEORY[3]

As noted in the previous sections, GST best describes organizational behavior in close to stable equilibrium states. It can also be described as a linear systems model; that is, behavior is directly proportional to the sum of relevant inputs. Linear systems generally are expressed by simple input–output relationships, and change tends to be easily regulated, orderly, and incremental. First-order change efforts are generally effective in organizational systems that are behaving in accordance with linear systems principles (i.e., as predicted by GST).

The GST model, however, is not as useful when dealing with organizational systems that are operating in environments that do not allow them to settle into comfortable patterns and cycles of dynamic equilibrium. When organizational systems are operating far from equilibrium, the environment becomes chaotic and demonstrates nonlinear features (Stacey, 1992; Stacey et al., 2000; Wheatley, 2006). In nonlinear systems, output responses are not directly proportional to inputs because the system response is not a simple sum of systems inputs. As many readers are aware, very strange things happen in nonlinear, far-from-equilibrium, chaotic environments. Small events produce very large and unpredictable results (the so-called butterfly effect; Butz, 1997; Lorenz, 1963). Systems characterized by nonlinear dynamics (e.g., weather) are notoriously difficult and require enormous computing power to predict.

An adequate treatment of chaos and complexity theory is not possible in this review. Some of the related principles from these theories, however, do have practical relevance to this discussion.

[3] Some of the text in this section is from "The History and Current Status of Organizational and Systems Change," by H. S. Leonard, in H. S. Leonard, R. Lewis, A. M. Freedman, and J. Passmore (Eds.), *The Wiley-Blackwell Handbook of the Psychology of Leadership, Change, and Organizational Development* (pp. 256–257), 2013, Wiley-Blackwell UK (https://doi.org/10.1002/9781118326404.ch12). Copyright 2013 by Wiley-Blackwell UK. Reprinted with permission.

1. It should be apparent to the reader, for instance, that first-order solutions are generally ineffective in nonlinear, chaotic environments. In fact, first-order solutions often make the situation worse (Watzlawick et al., 1974).
2. Second-order change (Bateson, 1972; Watzlawick et al., 1974) is necessary for organizational systems to operate effectively in chaotic environments. Because simple operating principles no longer work in chaotic environments, organizational members at all levels of the organization must be able and willing to examine governing principles, assumptions, goals, and values if they have any hope of dealing with unpredictable surprises that emerge.
3. The typical bureaucratic practices and policies that lead to predictability and stability become a liability when organizations need to be agile, creative, and innovative (Stacey, 1992). It is impossible to know what or who will be needed and necessary, and therefore even in the near future, organizations that rely on creativity and innovation (e.g., Apple, Google) purposely blur lines and levels of authority and power and give people time to play with ideas and concepts.
4. Chaotic environments place a premium on the ability of organizations to self-organize quickly rather than the ability to implement a long-term plan. Organizational charts become very fluid, and time horizons for strategic plans are shortened (Stacey et al., 2000).
5. In chaotic and highly complex environments, it is very hard to establish cause and effect (Stacey, 1992). By the time the organization fully understands what happened in the past, a new future is upon it. As Watzlawick et al. (1974) noted, a first-order analysis of *what* just happened—action and response—may be more useful than a comprehensive understanding of *why* it happened. An analysis of first-order cause and effect, combined with deft and rapid self-organization by management and employees, often carries the day in highly chaotic environments.
6. Systems dynamics in chaotic environments are highly sensitive to some changes but remarkably insensitive to others (Stacey, 1992). Moreover, it is devilishly difficult to predict which changes will result in huge versus minimal impact. Consequently, a flexible implementation

plan is usually preferable to strict adherence to a project plan in highly chaotic and unstable environments.[4]

7. Organizations in highly unstable markets or markets that require high levels of creativity may develop practices and policies that discourage stability and encourage chaos (Stacey, 1992). High levels of creativity, novelty, and self-organization are required when organizations operate in the highly dynamic and unpredictable border between order and chaos. Silicon Valley, outside of San Francisco, can be described as one such region where purposeful chaos can be useful.
8. Complex and chaotic environments place a premium on the development of organizational learning capabilities. Organizations cannot expect that a simple, linear path to their goals exists. Organizational members at all levels must be able to develop a workable understanding of complex dynamics and invent new solutions to novel and unprecedented challenges.

IMPLICATIONS FOR CONSULTING PRACTICE OF SYSTEMS THEORIES

Systems theories are seldom used directly as O/SC interventions. The various theories and models in this chapter provide a manual to explain how social and organizational systems work. Further, systems theories provide several extremely useful tools for analyzing any social or organizational system regardless of size or scale. A firm grounding in systems theory also builds a consultant's credibility with current and future clients.

Most organizational managers and leaders have been introduced to the importance of viewing their organization and its environment as a system with dynamic relationships between system elements. Most also recognize that there are characteristic patterns of interactions between system elements in certain circumstances. A more detailed and substantive understanding of systems theory will be useful in a number of ways.

[4] The reader is referred to Figure 4.3 for a more complete discussion of ideal versus realistic program implementation.

By demonstrating a sophisticated understanding of systems and how systems operate, organizational consultants build credibility and confidence in the recommendations for change that they propose. Here are some specific examples of how systems theory can be useful in O/SC.

Organizational Assessment or Analysis

Almost every change strategy begins with an analysis of the situation currently facing the organization. Systems theory, particularly GST, provides a comprehensive model of the key components of an organizational system as well as the fundamental and universal dynamics of energy and information flow through the systems. In addition to providing useful mental models and vocabulary, GST provides a useful "checklist" to make sure that all important elements of the organizational system are accounted for.

Whether consulting/coaching individual managers and leaders or leadership teams (see Schein, 1999), a firm and in-depth knowledge of organizational systems will help guide the conversations and discussions and suggest useful inquiries and questions. Following are a few examples.

Systems as Cycles of Events

Consultants can encourage leaders to systematically trace how information and energy move and are transformed within the organization—not only between subsystems but also between the organization and its environment. This process is analogous to the recommendation to "follow the money" in prosecuting cases of fraud and political malfeasance.

Primary Tasks

Consideration of an organization's primary task, a task that is critical to the survival of the enterprise, may seem obvious in most situations—it consists of the organization's principal products and services. In times of crisis, however, it may not be so obvious. The cases of Kodak, Xerox, and IBM demonstrate that technology or world events can upend well-established product lines and services and force deeper consideration about the organization's primary task. A well-placed and well-timed question from a consultant in strategic planning sessions or executive coaching sessions can have an enormous impact on deliberations about an organization's primary task.

Steady-State and Dynamic Equilibrium

It is often helpful to question why things don't change rather than describing why things should change. Lewin's (1943) force-field analysis process (see Figure 3.1) can be useful in these situations. In many cases, the consultant can help leaders understand that second-order change requiring fundamental questioning of assumptions and goals (Bateson, 1972; Kuhn, 1962/1996; Watzlawick et al., 1974), rather than traditional, first-order change as recommended in standard "best practices" recommendations, are required to solve persistent problems.

Systems Thinking

Reference to some of the "rules of thumb" about systems suggested by Senge (1990) can help leaders break out of linear thinking when planning change and, perhaps, anticipate a few unintended consequences of actions and decisions.

Chaos Theory

Helping organizational leaders understand the dynamics of organizations and systems operating far from system equilibrium (consider the political and economic situations in the United States in 2008 or 2020), as predicted by chaos theory, can be helpful and build confidence and credibility in the value of a consultant's services.

Content Presentations

Consultants are often contracted to design content presentations of various lengths to introduce systems theory in planning sessions and training sessions, often in leadership development programs. The various theories presented in this chapter are useful in developing mental models that help managers and leaders understand systems and how they can operate effectively within them.

While systems theory may not be employed directly in designing systems change interventions, it can be used in many ways to inform, explain, and manage a wide variety of O/SC interventions.

3

Lewinian, Organization Development, and Change Management

Lewin's early effort to use behavioral science theory to solve real, practical problems (Lewin, 1943, 1947, 1951) served as an inspiration for a whole generation of social and behavioral scientists immediately following World War II. Learning from efforts to change social systems, Lewin's students and those familiar with his work launched the experiential learning/laboratory education movement, which strongly influences "Western"[1] academic education and management/leadership training today. Many of this movement's well-known innovations, such as T-groups, flip-charts, feedback sessions, and team-building exercises, were developed at

[1] While the influence of the North American and European theory and practice is being challenged in some parts of the world, notably Asia, "Western" approaches are still highly influential and imitated throughout the world.

Portions of the text for this chapter are from "The History and Current Status of Organizational and Systems Change," by H. S. Leonard, in H. S. Leonard, R. Lewis, A. M. Freedman, and J. Passmore (Eds.), *The Wiley-Blackwell Handbook of the Psychology of Leadership, Change, and Organizational Development* (pp. 245–250), 2013, Wiley-Blackwell UK (https://doi.org/10.1002/9781118326404.ch12). Copyright 2013 by Wiley-Blackwell UK. Reprinted with permission.

https://doi.org/10.1037/0000328-003
Essential Strategies for Organizational and Systems Change: An Overview for Consultants, by H. S. Leonard, R. R. Kilburg, and A. M. Freedman

National Training Laboratories by Lewin's students and followers in the years and decades after his untimely death in 1947 (Bradford, 1967; Marrow, 1967). The roots for the organization and systems change approach that has been termed *organization development* (OD) are deeply embedded in this tradition (Bennis et al., 1969).

Lewin had initially been interested in going into medicine but later decided to study the related field of biology. When his interests shifted to psychology, he was strongly influenced by the Gestalt school that was popular in Germany at the time (Marrow, 1969). This approach applied a holistic/dynamic rather than a deterministic/reductionist approach to the study of perception and psychological experience (Boring, 1950).

In keeping with this tradition, he developed his field theory, which he applied to both personality and social systems that he viewed as different units of analysis in the psychological field (Lewin, 1951). For Lewin, behavior could not be understood solely by identifying a linear, causal sequence of precipitating events. To understand behavior, one needed to understand the relevant variables in the environment *at that time* as well as dynamic factors within the individual or individuals. He expressed this relationship as B = *fn* (P,E); that is, behavior is a function of the person and his or her environment (Lewin, 1943).

His well-known *force-field analysis* (Lewin, 1943; see Figure 3.1) is a good example of how this rather theoretical expression can be applied to very practical problems. Lewin reasoned that any behavior that showed stable characteristics must be in some form of dynamic equilibrium. Therefore, to change the behavior to a new behavior or a new level of the same behavior, the change agent needed to understand all the relevant forces driving new behavior as well as all relevant forces that were resisting any change in behavior. With this analysis completed, the change agent could either increase the driving forces or reduce the restraining forces, thereby eliminating the equilibrium. Lewin further argued and provided evidence that, as a general rule, reducing restraining forces was more effective than increasing driving forces in changing behavior in situations where individuals experience feelings of threat related to the desired change.

Lewin's field theory was a dramatic departure from the deterministic and reductionist psychoanalytic models of change that were popular at

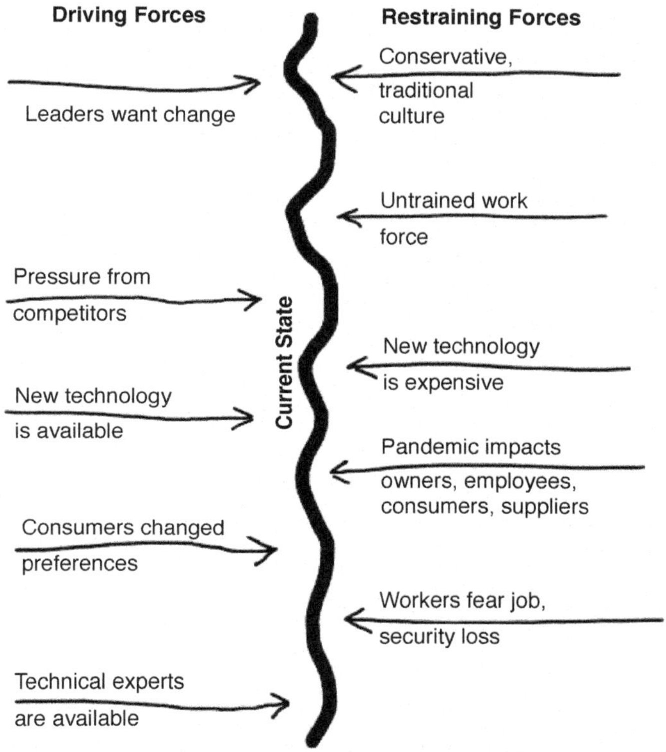

Figure 3.1

Note. Force-field analysis to assess the current state of the organization. Data from Lewin (1943).

the time. Unfortunately, Lewin died before he could further develop his ideas about change and social systems. Fortunately, his students (e.g., Ron Lippitt, Morton Deutsch, Leon Festinger, Bluma Zeigarnik, Maria Ovsiankina, Kate Lissner, Vera Mahler) did develop them. The field of study we now term *group dynamics* was inspired by Lewin and was largely developed by students and disciples of, or believers in, his principles of change (see Cartwright & Zander, 1968).

For Lewin, change was an experimental process that involved taking action based on existing theories and ideas, observing the results of the action, developing better models for understanding the behavior and making better predictions, and then modifying the change efforts accordingly. Lewin's model was a contemporaneous, forward-looking model based on action, an approach that was in contrast to the backward-looking, passive analysis of behavior that seemed to characterize psychoanalytic theory. This experimental, contemporaneous, forward-looking stance can be seen in many change strategies that were significantly influenced by Lewin, such as OD (Cummings & Worley, 2015), change management (Kotter, 1996), and Action Learning (Marquardt et al., 2009).

Further, while psychoanalytic models of behavior that prevailed during Lewin's time and the mid-20th century provided valuable understanding of the individual as well as the social dynamics of human behavior (Diamond, 1993; Freud, 1930/2005; Kets de Vries, 2006; Levinson, 2006), these theories relied primarily on increasing insight to change behavior. Lewin's action-based approach was a contrast to the rather passive change approaches developed by psychoanalytically inspired theorists. Lewin's model, therefore, was enthusiastically embraced by those who believed that rationally based, planned change strategies were ideally suited to bring about the social change campaigns that emerged in the mid-20th century (e.g., democratization of national politics and organizations, civil and human rights, and global economic development). Recognizing Lewin's contributions, many psychoanalytically grounded theorists also embraced his practice models for enacting organizational change (see Kilburg, 2000).

The following principles and practices of organization and social change can be traced back to Lewin and the influential Lewinian School of social psychology.

DATA-BASED DECISION MAKING, FEEDBACK, AND ACTION RESEARCH

Lewin's well-known dictum that "nothing is as practical as a good theory" (Marrow, 1969) not only demonstrated his belief in the practical as well as theoretical value of theory but also marked a pivot point in research in psychology and the behavioral sciences. Previous research in experimental psychology had been primarily conducted in a laboratory where researchers made careful efforts to control for all variables other than the one or two under study (see Boring, 1950). This approach violated Lewin's belief that research must study the normal environment in which an event or phenomenon occurs, methodology that is difficult or nearly impossible to achieve in a sterile experimental laboratory. At least in psychology,[2] Lewin is considered the father of what has been termed *field research*, the study of events or phenomenon in their natural environments.

Followers of Lewin, particularly in the field of OD, embraced his emphasis on the pragmatics of research in developing action research models and methods (Argyris, 1970; Greenwood & Levin, 1998; Lewin, 1946). In the action research approach, practical methods of research, including surveys and interviews of organizational employees, stakeholders, and clients as well as direct observation and analysis of behavioral data (French & Bell, 1984), are used. The action research method is reiterative and generally includes the following action cycle: (a) action planning to achieve a goal, (b) taking action, (c) assessing the effects of the action, (d) reflecting on the implications of the action, (e) making any necessary modifications to the initial action plan, and (f) taking action based upon the preceding analysis and modification of the plan (Freedman, 2006). Data collection and research is conducted in any stage in the cycle but particularly in Stages 1, 3, and 4.

Lewin believed that action-based research was the basis for purposeful and effective change, and this is reflected in his well-known statement: "No action without research; no research without action" (Marrow, 1969, p. 163).[3]

Herb Shepard and Wendell French, both early OD pioneers, emphasized that action research is purposeful research to guide present and

[2] There is a long history of field research in disciplines such as cultural anthropology (Burgess, 1984) and sociology (Durkheim, 1895/1982; Nisbet, 1967). In psychology, however, there are few examples of field research before Lewin. The current enthusiasm for qualitative research (Patton, 2002) can be traced back to Lewin.

[3] The reader may recognize the similarity of this quote by Reg Revans (1983), the father of Action Learning, that "there can be no action without learning and no learning with action" (p. 74). Revans was extending Lewin's statement of belief if it is accepted that the goal of research is increased learning.

future action (French & Bell, 1984). Simultaneous to guiding effective action, action research was also used to build the body of scientific knowledge. *Action* in this sense refers to "programs and interventions designed to solve problems and improve conditions" (French & Bell, 1995, p. 137).

The notion of feedback is particularly important in the action research model. The output and results of most academically oriented research is scholarly publication providing formal, and often technical, feedback for other scholars and the academic community. In contrast, the audience for the output or findings of action research is primarily for organizational decision makers and the change agents themselves.

Another philosophic as well as operational distinction between action research and academically oriented research is that the analysis of the data in action research is generally led by organizational members (employees as well as leadership) rather than by the researchers who gathered the data. The notion of "feedback loops" created by this feedback process is often associated with general systems theory or cybernetics (computer) theory. The feedback process, however, was observed and identified as a potent change strategy even earlier by Lewin (1946) as the result of an academic and community development conference to improve race relations in New Britain, Connecticut, after World War II. As a result of this early "action research," feedback loops and processes have been designed into virtually all OD or laboratory education processes since.

THE ROLE OF EXPERTS

The learnings from some of the earliest efforts to achieve social change began to challenge the primacy of experts and expert judgment. In the social change program in New Britain (Lewin, 1946), nonexpert community feedback that was first resisted by the experts (including Lewin) was judged, ultimately, to be crucial in understanding the phenomena they were experiencing and studying. The expert staff of this community change conference concluded that nonexpert feedback from community members improved planning and increased the effectiveness of future action.

Later, Revans (1983), the accepted "father" of Action Learning, went further by insisting that expert and nonexpert opinions be given equal importance in guiding the Action Learning process (see Chapter 5). Current practice for many Action Learning processes is to include participants with little or no prior knowledge of a subject or topic in developing solutions to problems. The assumption for this practice is that these people will be willing to ask "dumb" questions that those with more expertise would overlook or avoid. Action research and data feedback have served as the basis or backbone from the earliest beginnings of what has now been termed OD (Katzell, 1960; Shepard, 1960). Figure 3.2 displays the use of action research in a prototypical OD-based organizational and systems change (O/SC) consultation.

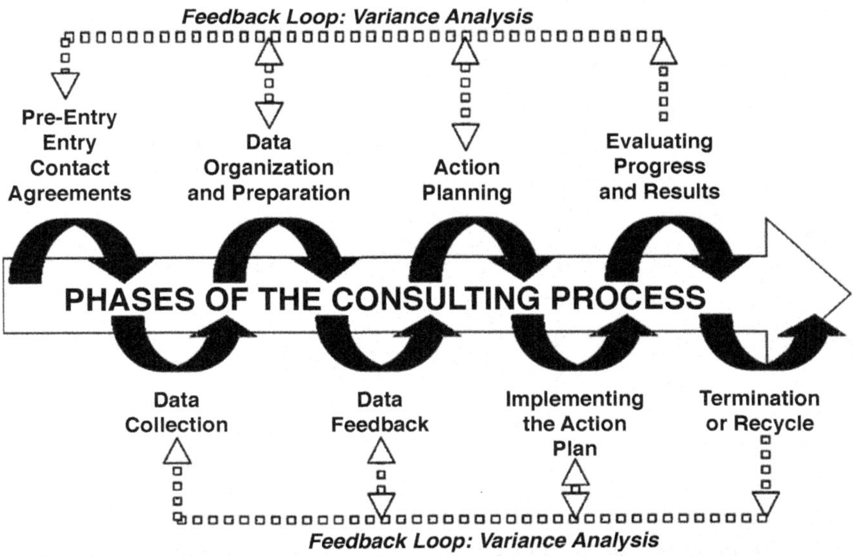

Figure 3.2

Note. Uses of action of action research, data collection, and data feedback in a typical organization development–based organizational and systems change process. Data from Lippitt and Lippitt (1986) and Block (2011).

UNFREEZING, CHANGING, AND REFREEZING CHANGE MODEL

The force-field analysis that has already been addressed in this chapter (Lewin, 1943) forms the basis for this fundamental change model. Once a force-field analysis has been completed, change agents can create an action plan to increase driving forces, reduce restraining forces, or combine these two approaches to "unfreeze" the current equilibrium or status quo. Based on his change experience, Lewin (1947) recommended an emphasis on reducing restraining forces when the issue involved significant elements of personal or organizational threat.

Once a new desired level or form of behavior is achieved, the change agent takes action to stabilize and achieve a new equilibrium. During the time that this model was developed, long periods of relative quiet and stability could be anticipated between organizational crises or change initiatives. As Vaill noted as early as 1996, this assumption of relatively smooth sailing between patches of "whitewater" no longer seemed valid. The pace of change and organizational disruption has only increased over the intervening years (Marquardt et al., 2009).

While the basic "unfreezing, changing, and refreezing" model has necessarily been modified over the years, it continues to be widely used in various forms by change management practitioners (see Kotter, 1996). Recognizing the increasing turbulence in the organizational environment, the general trend has been to split the larger action research cycle into changes with smaller scale and shorter time spans. Figure 3.3 provides a visual presentation of a realistic Action Research process in the context of expected turbulence.

PARTICIPATION IN PLANNING AND DECISION MAKING

One key principle in OD and change management methods is that participation in planning and decision making generates more engagement and ownership in the change process and, consequently, less resistance and more support for the change plan that is ultimately developed. This

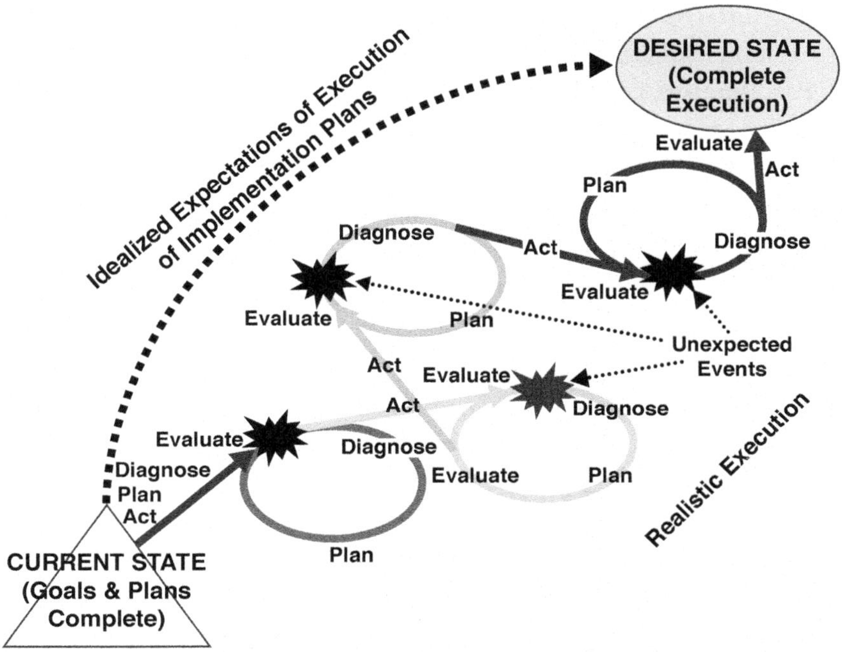

Figure 3.3

Note. Visual presentation of the action research process in a contemporary change initiative. Data from Lewin and Gold (1999).

strongly held principle was so well established by the mid-1960s that it was incorporated into Rensis Likert's System 4 (1967). This model was based on a series of studies using action research and survey feedback to affect organizational change conducted by the Survey Research Center at the University of Michigan. Likert (1967) consolidated and ranked organizations into four systems of management:

- **Exploitive authoritative (System 1)** exhibits an autocratic, top-down approach to leadership.
- **Benevolent authoritative (System 2)** is similar to System 1 except that management is more paternalistic.

- **Consultative (System 3)** involves more employee interaction, communication, and decision making.
- **Participative group (System 4)** is the opposite of System 1 and is designed around group decision making and supervision. This system promotes high degrees of member involvement and participation. Communication is both lateral and vertical, and decisions are linked by overlapping group membership (Likert, 1967).

This body of research and practice experience was also incorporated into Blake and Mouton's (1964) Management Grid approach (discussed later in this section) that was also built on a series of studies at the University of Michigan that strongly indicated two distinct but important elements of managerial behavior: (a) concern for production and (b) concern for people (Katz & Kahn, 1952).

Despite the strong belief that OD theorists and practitioners have in the causal link between participation ⇒ engagement ⇒ ownership ⇒ support for strategic change, until recently, limited evidence of direct relationships between these variables has been available (Lines, 2004). Lines, however, did report strong relationships between participation and five change outcomes: goal achievement, resistance to change, loyalty, effort, and identification. The adjusted R^2 (percentage accounted for by participation) ranged from .15 (effort) to .31 (resistance), and the related significance levels were all less than .001. This evidence provides strong and significant support for the faith that OD and change management practitioners and theorists place in this factor.

ATTITUDE FORMATION

One of Lewin's students, Leon Festinger, developed two principles that have gained great currency in OD and social psychology. The first was his notion of social reality (Festinger, 1954). Festinger demonstrated that what people considered "reality" was socially based. In other words, people use other people's perceptions in establishing what they consider to be real. He noted that this social comparison process often has more power and weight than actual measures of reality. The notion that "perception is reality" seems universally accepted now in large measure because of the work of Festinger and other social psychologists (e.g., Asch, 1951) in the 1950s and 1960s. This principle, along with the principle of feedback, serves as the basis for "360-degree surveys," which provide feedback to employees and managers from their subordinates, colleagues, customers, and bosses.

The other well-known principle developed by Festinger was his theory of cognitive dissonance (Festinger, 1957). This principle states that holding two inconsistent ideas at the same time leads to mental "tension," which causes one or both of the ideas to be modified to reduce this "cognitive dissonance." One implication of this principle is that changing behavior will also change attitudes when they are inconsistent with each other.

GROUP COHESIVENESS AND IDENTIFICATION

The power of group cohesiveness and identification had earlier been noted in the well-known Hawthorne effect (Mayo, 1949). One conclusion drawn from these studies was that production went up merely because of the focus of attention workers were receiving rather than because of any objective changes in working conditions. It was also noted, however, that production could be depressed because the pressures to increase production broke informal norms established by the team regarding a fair wage for their work. There seemed to be pressures for behavior conformity to resist "rate-busting." Schachter et al. (1951) provided additional experimental evidence for the power of team cohesiveness to either support or resist change efforts. The Hawthorne studies and later social psychological experiments demonstrated the importance of developing strong team cohesiveness and of getting the support of currently cohesive social units (e.g., organizational units and teams) in generating successful organizational change. One only has to observe the popularity and ubiquity of "team-building" events (discussed later in this chapter) to recognize the importance of group cohesiveness and identification.

BASES OF SOCIAL POWER

Central to the Lewinian approach to change is the notion that there are many social and physical sources of power at play in organizations, particularly in organizational politics. French and Raven (1968) were among the first to identify the various sources of social power: reward, coercive, legitimate, referent, and expert. These authors pointed to sources of social power that are often overlooked or taken for granted.

NATIONAL TRAINING LABORATORIES

Shortly after Lewin died in 1947, a number of his students and colleagues decided to create an experimental community or social laboratory devoted to the practical study of social behavior toward the practical end of improving social conditions, society, and the conditions that led to war, such as World War II. This social laboratory, first created at a small college preparatory school in Bethel, Maine, during the academic summer break in 1947, continues to this date (virtually in 2021 as a result of the COVID-19 pandemic).

The "laboratory education" process at National Training Laboratories (NTL; Bradford et al., 1964) can be seen as the start of experiential learning in the modern era. Instead of sitting in classrooms with chairs lined up in rows with participants listening to lectures given by professors, experts, and thought leaders, participants might sit on the floor in a circle discussing what was going on right then, how it affected group members, and what that might mean in a theoretical yet practical sense. This group process, termed a *T-group* (T stands for "training"), relied on personal development to foster social change. This process was modified for use in organizations and corporations where it often was offered as "sensitivity training." The implicit assumption was that changes in leadership behavior (i.e., more sensitivity to the impact on employees) would result in positive changes in organizational performance (Golembiewski & Blumberg, 1970).

ORGANIZATION DEVELOPMENT

The limited impact of laboratory education (e.g., T-groups; Campbell & Dunnette, 1968), which was focused on personal development at the organizational and team level, led to the development of new methodologies.

At the organizational level, change efforts were research-focused at first, based on the action research model with dependent or outcomes variables such as organizational improvement (Katzell, 1960), organizational effectiveness (Argyris, 1962), and organization renewal (Lippitt, 1969). Although Argyris (1962) and others had used the term *organization development*, it wasn't generally accepted as an umbrella term until Beckhard (1969) published a book with that term in the title in the highly influential Addison-Wesley OD series of shorter, topic-focused books.

Following are several OD principles, practices, and tools that have been useful in the conduct of O/SC.

Humanism and O/SC

Maslow

Well known for his hierarchy of needs, Maslow (1954) posited that basic human needs such as air, food and water, and safety must be satisfied before higher psychological needs such as self-esteem and even higher self-fulfillment needs, described as self-actualizing needs, become important to people.

Theory X and Theory Y

McGregor (1960), a close associate of Maslow, applied Maslow's humanistic principles to motivation in organizations. McGregor described two management styles that make quite different assumptions about what motivates employees. Managers believing Theory X assume that most employees are motivated by extrinsic rewards such as salary, penalties, and sanction; have little interest in working creatively; and respond best to close and direct supervision. In contrast, managers believing Theory Y assume that employees are self-motivating, work better with more autonomy, and often seek jobs that are challenging and personally rewarding.

McGregor believed that managers with a strong Theory X bias inhibit higher enterprise-related performance, which leads to reduced job performance and increased turnover. While McGregor never argued for adopting a Theory Y approach in every situation (Maslow's theory would argue that there is a time and place for applying Theory X principles), his ideas gained increasing acceptance as companies pushed for peak performance in employees, high-performance teamwork, and greater employee and team creativity and autonomy. As you would expect, there is high acceptance of Theory Y in high-tech organizational environments such as Silicon Valley. Moreover, some organizations, such as the armed forces, that have traditionally assumed a Theory X belief regarding human motivation have adopted some Theory Y practices in situations that require creativity, initiative, and strong problem-solving skills such as after-action reviews (Cronin & Andrews, 2009; Sawyer & Deering, 2013).

Grid Theory

Building on the work of Maslow (1954) and McGregor (1960), Blake and Mouton (1964) proposed that the most effective management or leadership style demonstrated as much concern for the welfare of employees as concern for task accomplishment and financial results. Eschewing a middle-of-the-road approach that tried to balance concern for the task with concern for people, Blake and Mouton proposed that the best organizational performance could be achieved by meeting basic needs while engaging intrinsic needs for achievement, creativity, and high performance and also maintaining high standards and expectations for organizational results.

Blake and Mouton (1964) developed a well-structured organizational change program, based on grid theory, with two principal objectives: (a) developing a logic-based strategy for creating organizational excellence and (b) providing managers and leaders with the necessary knowledge and skills to achieve high performance by placing priorities on the welfare of employees as well as task performance (Cummings & Worley, 2015).

Team Building

The research-focused theories of group dynamics (Bales, 1970; Cartwright & Zander, 1968; Thelen, 1954) and team development (Bennis & Shepard, 1956; Gibbard et al., 1974; Tuckman, 1965) of the 1950s and 1960s were the basis for developing team-building methodologies (Dyer, 1987; Patten, 1981). In many cases, these team-building processes were repurposed "icebreaker," "warm-up," or experiential exercises designed to demonstrate key human relations principles and theories used in T-group and other laboratory education programs. Pfeiffer and Jones (1969–1986) edited a series of books filled with structured exercises that could be used as icebreakers for team and organizational meetings or for demonstrating key principles of social psychology such as feedback, self-disclosure, trust, and verbal and nonverbal communications.

Group and Team Facilitation

The nondirective and process-focused facilitation process developed at NTL and popularized by Carl Rogers (1965b, 1970; an NTL alumnus) was modified to be used in a host of situations including business meeting facilitation, strategic planning sessions, and experiential learning programs. Process facilitation is a core skill for many consultants working as organizational consultants (Hunter et al., 1995; Schwarz, 2002).

Process Consultation

Schein (1999) introduced process consultation in the Addison-Wesley OD series. He applied his theories and understanding of experiential learning, action research, and culture—specifically organizational culture—to what he termed *process consultation*. Schein (1999) defined organizational consultation as a process of helping the client organization to learn about itself and what it needed to do to become successful. He proposed that a facilitative/helping relationship was more effective than a prescriptive/expert (selling and telling) relationship. Schein (1999) noted that the process consultation approach is based on a number of principles that align well with OD principles:

1. Always try to be helpful. Every contact should be perceived as helpful.
2. Always stay in touch with the current reality. In this instance, Schein was referring to the psychologically based social reality that Festinger (1954) referred to.
3. Access your ignorance. It is not possible to understand the client's current reality without asking questions that reveal your ignorance about the client's situation.

4. Everything you do is an intervention and has consequences for the client.
5. It is the client who owns the problem and the solution. This is, perhaps, the most important of Schein's principles for management consultants. The client must be able to own the problem and fully engage in developing a solution. A corollary to this principle is that if you are working harder to solve the client's problem than the client is, you are not likely to be helpful to the client or successful as a consultant. (Schein, 1999, pp. 243–244)

OD and Planned Change

Richard Beckhard (1969) defined OD as organizational change efforts that were (a) planned, (b) organization-wide, (c) managed from the top, and designed to (d) increase organization effectiveness and health through (e) planned interventions in the organization's "processes," using knowledge based on behavioral science. While feedback and participation in change efforts from stakeholders throughout the organization were sought and encouraged, this definition acknowledged that the change efforts were to be managed from the top of the organization. This is a continuation of the change strategy employed by earlier organizational change approaches (Bennis et al., 1969). This definition also makes it clear that both organizational effectiveness and employee health have equal priority as objectives for OD interventions. Finally, this definition emphasizes that action must be based on behavioral science, including data and knowledge derived from action research efforts.

To support rational organizational planning, Beckhard and Harris (1987) proposed that the OD design start with a strategic analysis of the current condition of the organization (i.e., the current state) as well as a vision of desired state for the organization (i.e., the future state). Beckhard and Harris proposed that this information would be very useful in developing the OD goals as well as strategies. Figure 3.4 provides a flow chart for using these concepts and analyses to guide development of plans and implementation strategies.

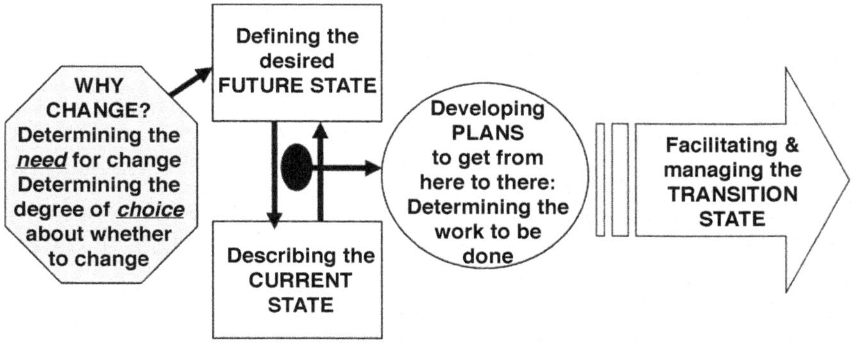

Figure 3.4

Note. Flow chart for strategic planning for organizational change. Data from Beckhard and Harris (1987).

Assessing an Organization's Readiness to Change

One of the earliest challenges faced by organizational consultants is determining when an organizational client is ready to commit to significant changes in the way it operates. Building on a formula delineated by Beckhard and Harris (1987),[4] Freedman (2017), with Jules, proposed the following equation that provides a comprehensive overview and roadmap for planning and implementing changes in complex organizations. The elaborated formula is

$$C = D \times V \times DS \times CS \times S \times I > MC + OC + PS,$$

where C means change, D is dissatisfaction, V is vision, DS is desired state, CS is current state, S is support, and I is incentives. MC refers to monetary costs, OC is opportunity costs, and PS is psychological costs.

Numerical values (e.g., from 0 to 5) may be assigned to each function based on leaders' assessment of the quality and comprehensiveness of each function. The total product is multiplicative. Thus, if any single function has a value of "0," the total product is "0." Furthermore, leadership should

[4] Beckhard and Harris (1987) acknowledged credit for the original formula belonged to David Gleicher, who developed the model while working at the accounting firm Arthur D. Little.

assign values to each of the three types of costs based on their judgment. The formula's multiplicative product must be greater than the additive value of MC + OC + PS.

When there is a large gap between the formula's product (i.e., D × V × DS × CS × S × I) and the total of costs (i.e., MC + OC + PS), it follows that efforts to deal with a change will cause little, if any, stress, strain, and tension in the organizational system. However, as the gap shrinks, the levels of stress, strain, and tension will increase—sometimes dramatically. When the product of the formula is estimated to be less than the sum of the costs, leaders are likely to terminate consideration of the radical change and keep things as they have been. This may be a wise decision, or it could mean the organization will allow itself to be swamped by changing, subject to adverse environmental conditions for which they remain unprepared. It should also be noted that when the perceived need for change greatly exceeds the perceived costs in this equation, the organization is likely to be in a state far distant from dynamic equilibrium. In this case, principles of chaos theory (see Chapter 2) will have significant relevance when planning or executing radical change in an organizational system.

This formula allows leaders to assess the probability of success for any particular change goal whether the change is simple or radical (see Chapter 4). It is also scalable. That is, leadership at any organizational level can apply it to plan simple changes or to implement radical changes at the individual, team, any subsystem (such as departments or regions), any combination of interdependent subsystems, or total organizational systems levels.

OTHER ORGANIZATIONAL CHANGE STRATEGIES INFLUENCED BY LEWIN

Efforts to improve organizational performance began in earnest with the action research programs of the late 1940s and 1950s. The OD strategy used data from action research for action planning and implementation. Business schools included OD and systems concepts in their curriculum. In fact, many organizational psychologists were recruited by business schools beginning in the late 1960s.

Change Management

Beginning in the 1990s, large accounting firms recognized the demand for organizational change consultation and began offering their own variant of OD that was marketed under the term *change management* (CM). Kotter (2012), a professor at the Harvard Business School, proposed an eight-step process (2012) with many common components of the Freedman and Jules model (Freedman, 2017) for planning and managing large organizational change programs:

- Establishing a Sense of Urgency
- Creating a Guiding Coalition
- Developing a Vision and Initiatives
- Communicating the Change Vision
- Empowering Employees for Broad-Based Action
- Generating Short-Term Wins
- Consolidating Gains and Producing More Changes
- Anchoring New Approaches in the Culture

Quality Circles

Although not a direct result of the NTL-inspired group dynamics and action research process, the quality circle approach is based on a number of similar principles. Following World War II, Japanese industrial products were generally of low quality. Edward Deming, an American engineer and statistician, consulted to Japanese industry and proposed a statistical process control system (Deming & Orsini, 2012) to improve the quality of Japanese products. An outgrowth of this consultation was the creation of the quality circle process (Ishikawa, 1980).

Quality circles comprise teams of three to 12 employees who do the same or similar work. Led by supervisors or managers, the teams meet regularly to identify, analyze, and eliminate work-related problems using statistical analysis tools. Although the teams use formal problem analysis tools, they are given freedom to choose what aspects of the problem to focus on. The quality circle process demonstrates a blend of the informal process typical of the T-group process and the more structured approach to problem solving that is typical of Action Learning teams.

CONTEMPORARY OD AND CM APPROACHES TO O/SC

Definitions

Consultants and consulting firms typically refer to CM rather than OD when describing their services and rarely refer directly to the Lewinian heritage of their practices. Because CM is so widely taught in business schools, it is part of the shared language for managers and executives schooled in business. The practices of some consultants and consulting firms, in fact, share little conceptual foundation with Lewin and classic OD process. CM practices that do trace their lineage to Lewin identify OD as (a) a planned effort, (b) organization wide, (c) managed from the top, and (d) focused on increasing organizational effectiveness and health (Davenport, 1995).

This Lewinian definition of OD supports a surprisingly broad scope of consulting activities. Harvard's Center for Workplace Development (2021) lists the following OD services: change management; culture change; before and after-action review; diversity, inclusion, and belonging; engagement, coaching, and executive onboarding or leadership transition; innovation; organizational assessment and organizational design; senior team effectiveness; strategy development; and succession planning.

OD/CM Practitioners

Skilled OD/CM practitioners often work alone or in small consultancies. Most elite management consulting firms have CM practices (e.g., Boston Consulting Group, Bain & Company, McKinsey & Company). In addition, most of the major national and international accounting, financial, and human capital management firms also have substantial CM practices (e.g., Deloitte, PWC, KPMG, Accenture, Mercer, Korn Ferry). In many cases, CM practices and principles are integrated into traditional business consulting practices as firms diversify into the lucrative organizational change market. The core business for these consulting firms is often closely tied to the business service the company traditionally provided (i.e., Accenture, accounting; Korn Ferry, recruiting; Right Management, outplacement; Deloitte, technology transformation).

THE TINYpulse STORY—A CASE EXAMPLE

TINYpulse (TP) provides anonymous feedback to companies regarding the level and quality of engagement of their employees with their employers and their work. David Niu, the founder, has an international background, having been born in Taiwan and raised in the U.S. Midwest; a strong background in business and international development (University of California–Berkeley and Wharton); and an early experience with business development and technology, starting his first technology-based company while in graduate school.

After interviewing executives of growing and thriving companies (mostly small service and start-up organizations), Niu concluded that the success of these organizations was closely tied to the connection between the company and its employees as well as the culture developed and nurtured by senior leadership. He identified employee engagement with the company, their work, and the mission of their employer as key success factors for these companies (Niu, 2021). A corollary of this key insight is that real-time and targeted information about employee feelings and views regarding their company and their work would yield a substantial competitive advantage for these organizations.

Niu had the background and tools to operationalize this insight by creating a tool that allowed companies to keep a "finger on the pulse" of their enterprise. He had a sophisticated understanding of organizational management, growth, and change through his business education; firsthand and practical experience in starting and managing the growth of businesses; and the technological understanding, resources, and connection to create the process tools he envisioned. His company provides anonymous feedback by asking employees to answer a small set of questions about their feelings of work engagement and satisfaction on a frequent and regular basis. TP uses the latest cloud-based technology to guarantee the anonymity for respondents, which increases the level of trust and security among poll takers. TP's current clients include Microsoft, Sony, and the U.S. government.

Elora Voyles, an industrial–organizational psychologist and chief people scientist for TP, traces the firm's change strategy back to Lewin (Lewin & Gold, 1999) and describes it as being aligned and consistent with Kotter's (1996) CM model. TP outlines its change process as follows: (a) define future state, outcomes, and results; (b) assess current state and readiness; (c) design a change management team; (d) implement and mentor the plan; (e) stabilize the change; and (f) evaluate mid- and long-term results.

TP consults with human relations and OD departments or sections in client organizations to provide the necessary organization structure, culture, and processes for organizational change by setting a tangible and realistic vision; embracing change management; getting constant feedback from teams and employees; using the right tools; leading the project with top leadership skills; and communicating as effectively as possible. If requested, TP provides direct CM consulting as well as the necessary organization research (i.e., survey design and validation, training) and implementation management to support TP principles as essential CM processes.

IMPLICATIONS OF LEWINIAN CHANGE FOR APPROACHES TO O/SC CONSULTATION

Lewin's field theory and numerous models for O/SC are the foundation of modern OD practice. His force-field analysis is commonly used for analyzing the dynamic forces that encourage and resist efforts to change organizations. Principles of action research are critical for gathering the kind of practical data that are crucial for planning and managing change.

After Lewin's untimely death, his students went on to develop laboratory education, laying out the key principles of group dynamics and group development that provided the foundation for a whole host of consulting interventions including T-groups and sensitivity training, grid theory, Systems 4, team building, team facilitation, process consultation, and change management. In addition to being recognized as the father of contemporary social psychology, Lewin is also responsible for inspiring the experiential learning movement described in Chapter 6.

4

Leading and Managing Radical Change

From late 2019 through the writing of this chapter, the world has been thrown into a distressing, destabilizing condition due to the COVID-19 pandemic. This has been exacerbated by localized civil disruptions of various kinds. These conditions are affecting governments, large and small businesses, infrastructure, and nonprofit organizations. Organizational leaders are confronted with the need to plan and implement internal systemic changes in response to these changing external events and circumstances. Some of these are relatively small, incremental changes, like an upgrade in a computer program. These require a small learning curve and can be solved using first-order change (see Chapter 2). Some other external changes require a significant but manageable adaptation, like an upturn or downturn in volume of sales and delivery of goods or services, which, in turn, require an increase or decrease in the labor force. Relatively few external changes are totally discontinuous with past experience

https://doi.org/10.1037/0000328-004
Essential Strategies for Organizational and Systems Change: An Overview for Consultants, by H. S. Leonard, R. R. Kilburg, and A. M. Freedman

and require radical internal changes. For example, these occur in response to such catastrophic events as the widespread and deadly COVID-19 pandemic, massive hurricanes, and social disruptions, with or without accompanying economic depression.

When confronted by such discontinuities, organizations of all types, as well as the larger society, are unlikely to return to the old or a "new normal" any time soon, if at all. Organizations, governmental systems, and society as a whole may be reaching a number of simultaneous tipping points (Gladwell, 2000). The need for making such radical changes requires the second-order change approaches discussed in Chapter 2. Change principles suggested by chaos theory research (Chapter 2) also become relevant.

These are not the only radical external impacts on organizations (Bazerman & Watkins, 2008). For example, organizations face increasing competitive pressure, and computerization and robotic automation impact many industrial organizations and displace many unskilled and semi-skilled workers. Some companies are benefiting from these multiple phenomena. For example, those whose technological innovations enable people to work at home are thriving.

These challenges consist of one or more configurations of problems to solve, opportunities to exploit, and dilemmas to manage. The increasing challenge seems to be how leaders of large and small businesses, government agencies, and nonprofits will plan and implement radical changes in their complex organizations in a complicated environment.

Organizational leaders may be overwhelmed by these extraordinary demands. To meet these challenges, consultants, as trusted advisors, need to provide leadership with practical socio-technical-cultural systems-based models for achieving radical change. Organizations may be tempted to hire organizational consultants who promise simple and logical-sounding solutions based on many of the practices documented in this chapter.

Many large and successful consulting firms have one basic change model that they sell to organizations in any situation (e.g., McKinsey's 7S Framework; Channon & Cooper, 2015). In effect, these consultancies argue that all organizational problems and challenges can be addressed and solved using the same generic change strategy framework. Many management consultants base their contract negotiations with prospective client systems, as well as their change strategies and tactics, on a rather simplistic, often implicit, model in which a desirable future quickly rises from the ashes of the preexisting system (Freedman, 1997). Given the permutations and combinations of circumstances, system configurations, resources, and other factors, these simplistic solutions are unlikely to result in the radical, second-order changes that these organizations and systems require.

THE PHOENIX AND SWAMP MODELS

Freedman (2017) proposed the Phoenix model, which is a reasonable but unrealistic basis for planning radical change. In selecting a strategy and tactical goals and then developing plans of action, leaders benefit from considering a realistic understanding of the radical change process. This Phoenix model (see Figure 4.1) is reasonable in that it seems logical. But it is unrealistic even though it is what many organizational leaders naively

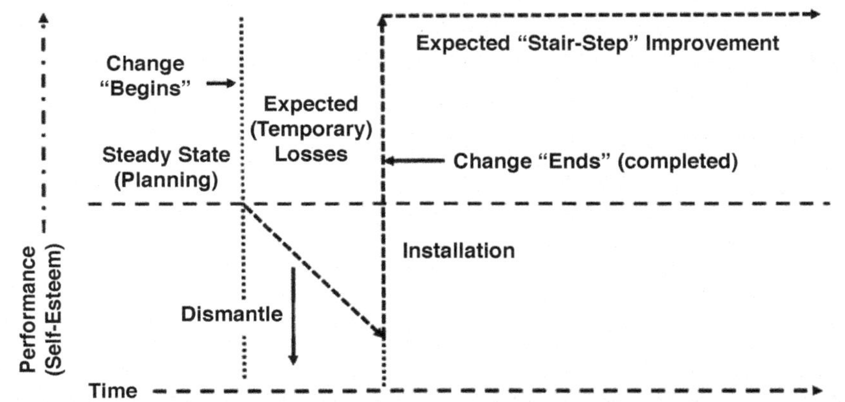

Figure 4.1

Note. The phoenix model—the reasonable change model. Adapted from *Leading Radical Change in Complex Organizations: A Field Book* (p. 76), by A. M. Freedman, 2017, ClearSpace. Copyright 2017 by ClearSpace. Adapted with permission.

want to believe because it promises maximum gains at minimum disruption, discomfort, and cost.

The reasonable but unrealistic notion is that a period of planning for change is initiated that precedes the start of a change process. During planning, the Phoenix model suggests that systemic performance will remain at a dissatisfying, but moderate, level, as will the confidence and self-esteem of the leaders and members of the organization. When change begins, parts or all of the preexisting system will be dismantled as the new parts are quickly installed. During this time of disruption, there will be expected, but temporary, losses in performance, confidence, and self-esteem. People will doubt their capacity to adapt and master the demands of the changes. However, the belief is that when the installation is complete, leaders and members will quickly master the demands created by the change, and there will be a stairstep improvement in performance, confidence, and self-esteem. It is further believed that the period during which dismantling and installation take place will be brief. Also, the new level of performance is expected to be significantly higher than the prechange level.

Consultants and coaches need to make sure that leaders appreciate the complexities and dynamics of their own organizational system. It is wise for these trusted advisors to use a practical sociotechnical systems model, termed the Swamp model, as a guide for explaining these complexities and dynamics to leaders who, too often, focus on their own areas of responsibilities without a great deal of attention to their areas' interdependencies and transactions with others' areas. This Swamp model can be traced back to von Bertalanffy's (1969) general systems concepts and Lewin (1943; see Figure 2.1).

According to the Swamp model (Figure 4.2), organizations take in essential resources from input-side stakeholders, such as suppliers, regulators, investors, markets, competitors, and scientific innovations. These resources are taken in through boundary management mechanisms or functions that are directly or indirectly tied to one or more specialized subsystems. There are six major subsystems: strategic direction (including legal services), human resource or human capital management, organizational structural management, financial management, technological

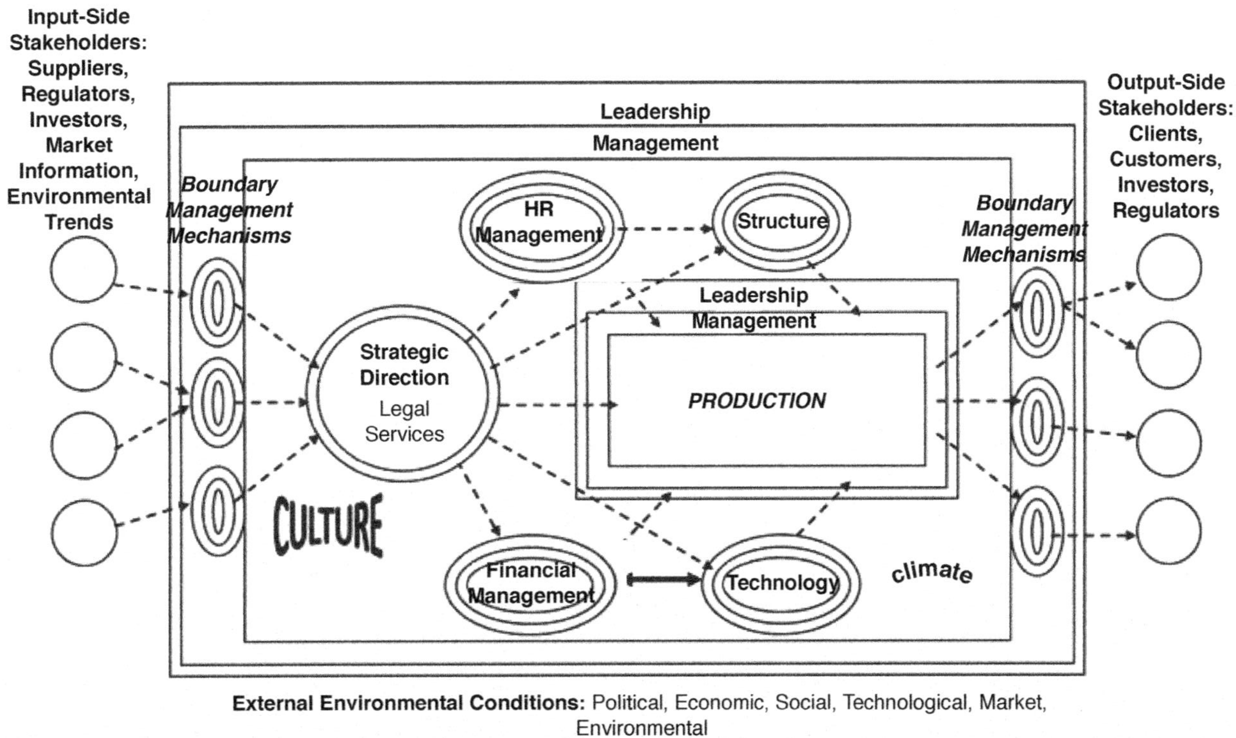

Figure 4.2

Note. The swamp model: a socio-technical-cultural model of organization. Adapted from *Leading Radical Change in Complex Organizations: A Field Book* (p. 95), by A. M. Freedman, 2017, ClearSpace. Copyright 2017 by ClearSpace. Adapted with permission.

management, and production. These subsystems are embedded in the organization's culture and affected by the organization's current emotional climate.

The organization's exports are managed by a second set of boundary management mechanisms that are tied to one or more external stakeholder groups. The output-side stakeholders are clients, customers, investors, regulators, and various specialists. The subsystems are all affected by the culture and climate and, in turn, contribute to the creation of the culture as well as the current climate. Each subsystem and boundary management mechanism is surrounded by its management and leadership (often, but not always differentiated). Executive leadership must accept responsibility for ensuring that a variance analysis function is in place and working. That is, they must make sure that each subsystem and their lateral interface transactions (i.e., inputs and outputs) are functioning as intended.

The entire organizational system is surrounded by its senior management and leadership. The primary relevant external environmental conditions are political, economic, social, technological, market, and environmental. Each boundary management mechanism and subsystem is directly or secondarily interrelated to and interdependent from all other systemic elements.

The dynamics of this complex mix of a system's component processes and behaviors makes a smooth transition from the current state to desired state unlikely. To help consultants and coaches understand and predict organizational behavior, the Swamp model can be used as a guide in their work with organizational leaders and managers at all levels. It will help to make sense of and organize the multitude and variety of information that consultants and coaches have to process.

COMPLEX SYSTEMS CHANGE STRATEGIES

Leaders must manage their own expectations—as well as those of their organizations' members—before, during, and after radical changes are initiated. It is unlikely that assimilation of and adaptation to a radical change will be a "V-shaped" recovery, as suggested by the Phoenix model. After all, organizational conditions following the radical change are unlikely to be at all similar to the pre–radical change conditions. Over time, radical organizational changes are likely to cycle through periods of incremental change alternating in an irregular pattern (Freedman, 2017; Nadler & Tushman, 1995).

Incremental change is characterized by comparatively low levels of activity, intensity, and complexity. This allows leadership more time with access to more resources to cope with the demands for change. Periods of radical change are characterized by elevated levels of activity, intensity, and complexity. With high intensity, such as arbitrary and short deadlines for completion of some actions, there is a high probability of discontinuity leading to dislocation, disruption, trauma, stress, strain, tension, and psychological pain. High levels of complexity refer to the involvement of a large number and variety of organizational parts and elements that are involved in or affected by the radical change.

Nadler and Tushman (1995) proposed that at the lowest level of intensity and complexity, change is not likely to be radically disruptive and can be managed through normal managerial processes. At moderate levels of intensity and complexity, change can be managed through delegation—for example, by assigning the change management function to a transition management team. At the highest levels of intensity and complexity, radical change must be led by a visible, unified, vocal team of executive and senior leaders and managers who are fully committed to making the radical change work for the entire organization.

A common error leaders make is to assume that radical changes can be managed through normal management processes. In such instances, normal management becomes overloaded with unfamiliar responsibilities for which people are unprepared. When leaders expect fluctuations, they can manage the expectations of their organizational members in a positive manner, thus minimizing stress and tension.

Basically, there are four likely strategies (Freedman, 2017) for designing methods for managing radical change. The first is a limited, defined pilot project in which the radical changes are introduced into a single work unit. This can be studied as the radical change is implemented to determine what, if any, adverse side effects or unexpected consequences emerge as well as the effectiveness of efforts to ameliorate those results. The second would be to introduce the radical change to an entire subsystem, like a region or product group. The third strategy would introduce incremental elements of the radical change to the entire organizational system sequentially, while noting how well organizational members adapted to each increment as well as emerging adverse side effects and the effectiveness of amelioration efforts. The fourth strategy has been called the *big bang* approach, in which the radical change is introduced to the entire organization at the same time—again noting emerging adverse reactions and the effectiveness of amelioration efforts. A mix of these strategies can be employed. For example, the first strategy may feed into the second or third, which may be followed by the fourth.

PHASES OF RADICAL CHANGE

Regardless of the scope of the radical change, the most realistic pattern that unfolds consists of four distinct, but often overlapping, phases (Freedman, 2017). When leaders expect fluctuations in emotions and performance, they can manage the expectations of their organizational members in a positive manner, thus minimizing stress and tension. Keeping the four phases of radical change in mind will alert leaders to probable fluctuations.

Phase I: Impact and Shock

The Nature of the Impact

The first of four phases occurs after planning and begins as action plans are initiated. It can be described as shock or impact as organizational members and stakeholders become aware of the adverse impacts of the radical change on their activities and their lack of capacity to cope with these demands. The first step of any innovative process is an act of destruction—that is, the destruction of the previous, well-known, predictable realities.

Time Span

This is a short-lived phase, lasting only hours for individuals and days for affected teams and subsystems. Different people and work units are likely to be at different places on different learning and adapting curves (Gladwell, 2000). Some are confident and stand at the forefront of innovations, and some are early adopters and supporters of the radical change. Others are part of a late majority or are laggards. A few are active or passive opponents of the radical change.

Emotions

It is extremely important that leaders at all organizational levels understand and legitimize the emotions that are likely to be elicited. That is, many people are likely to experience terror or panic, confusion, restlessness, and suspicion (Hansell, 1976). Increased individual, random activity is also likely to contribute to reduced operational effectiveness.

Protective Mechanisms

To protect themselves from the pain of these emotional consequences, people are likely to employ various protective mechanisms. Anger, which is quite common in Phase I, is intended to frighten or destroy perceived threats. Some people may insist on forceful, autocratic leadership that, they hope, will protect them and reestablish a sense of law and order. Also, some people may follow instructions to the letter. This verbatim compliance is likely to be a hostile response to leaders who are thought to be letting the organizational members down.

Leaders' Judgments

These may be biased, as leaders are tempted to discount emerging discontinuities. They may discount the need for fundamental, radical change and strive to adhere, as much as possible, to the previous status quo. They may defend themselves against disturbing anxiety and fear of radical change. They may want to avoid disrupting the previous existing equilibrium and power balance; they may want to avoid sacrifices. Whatever their anxieties, they will likely exude optimism about the future to allay the fears of their followers. This optimism is likely to be excessive, unsupported, and unrealistic. It is also likely to be short-lived as the realities of radical change become evident and inescapable for most involved parties.

Impacts on Structure

The organizing structure of systems deteriorates. There emerges an extreme range of unpredictable, nonaligned performance among members. A laissez-faire culture becomes evident, wherein individuals act independently, without coherent leadership and without consequences. Policies, procedures, rules, and regulations are constantly reinvented on an ad hoc basis. Formality is ignored. Signs and symptoms of low levels of conflict become evident. Many leaders and members are likely to deny the multiple impacts of radical change. This denial makes them vulnerable to be surprised and unable to adapt quickly.

Goal Setting and Planning

These activities tend to be expedient. The organization's mission is often ignored because the effort is to relieve the pain of immediate conditions. Strategic plans are ignored. Leaders and members also ignore their organization's values and philosophy. People neglect the relationship between their short-term, uncoordinated objectives; precipitous actions; and adverse consequences.

Several phenomena become evident during Phase I. First, goal setting and planning may seem irrelevant or lie dormant because the focus is on taking immediate, knee-jerk actions. Second, despite evident interdependencies, interface relations deteriorate. Members become concerned for themselves and their own group and its members. They are suspicious of other groups. There is considerable distancing from other groups, creating a functional disconnect.

Organizational and Political Barriers

There are several potential organizational and political barriers to an honest appreciation of the ramifications of radical change. Realistic leadership requires vision and courage that is often lacking among leaders who have not previously experienced radical changes. Further, fundamental, radical change often threatens the vested interests of various internal and external stakeholders who may offer leaders inducements for concessions that, if granted, would water down or simplify tactical plans. Making this picture more complicated, leaders tend to avoid rather than make overt conflict public.

Realistic Leadership

Leaders and their trusted advisors should intervene during Phase I by limiting excessive workloads, limiting emotional contamination, preserving the integrity of functional subsystems, and inducing hope in the future and faith in themselves. Specifically, leaders and their consultants should regulate the onset of changes and members' responses to radical change. Leaders should consider which overall strategy to employ (as discussed earlier). They should avoid surprises. They must develop mechanisms to create clarity among members. They must provide sufficient information to reduce the sense of strangeness. They must emphasize the need to achieve modest goals. And they must insist that the human resources function updates rules, regulations, policies, and procedures as often as it becomes evident that these adjustments are needed. One single, all-encompassing alteration will not suffice.

Leaders and their consultants must adopt an attitude that demonstrates they are extremely curious about and interested in members' reactions to radical change. While remaining passive, they must be prepared to be very responsive to members' evident and expressed needs and emotions. They must be very receptive to members' communications. Under no circumstances should leaders or consultants make any jokes about current conditions.

Leadership must take responsibility for creating and repetitively publicizing a compelling, attractive, desirable, and realistic vision of an achievable future for their organizations (Freedman, 2017). The vision must make sense to all organizational members as well as the organizations' internal and external stakeholders. It must be credible so stakeholders and organizational members recognize that achieving the vision would be beneficial to them.

Phase II: Defensive Retreat or Recoil and Turmoil

Time Span and the Nature of the Impact

Phase II lasts for several days for individuals and weeks for teams, subsystems, and interdependent subsystems as well as for external stakeholders that are integral elements of the organization's supply and delivery chains (Freedman, 1997, 2017). Phase II is characterized by a sharp decrease in performance and self-esteem as members discover that their preexisting skill sets are insufficient to cope with the demands of the radical change. Thus, organizational members and their leaders experience a sharp increase in frustration and dissatisfaction with themselves and others.

People wish and search for a heroic, charismatic leader (see Bion, 1961/1989) who can relieve the stress and tension they all experience. They want to find a strong parental figure who is stern, almost militaristic; who has a credible technocratic background; who conveys an autocratic image; and who strongly conveys their belief that they know what to do, who should do what, and how they should do it. However, such performances are likely to be hollow.

Impacts on Structure

System structure becomes steeply hierarchical. In their search for safety, leaders tend to rely on that which has been "tried and true." To demonstrate that they are dealing with visible but minor and temporary organizational perturbations, leaders are likely to establish permanent, but usually counterproductive, vertical command and control structures.

Conflict

As people try to adapt to radical change conditions and as they realize that established policies, procedures, rules, and regulations fail to help them to cope, signs and symptoms of moderate levels of conflict emerge. For example, in team meetings, detailed, time-consuming, wasteful digressive discussions become common. Unproductive competition becomes observable. The result is that teams, especially executive teams, fail to reach consensus on decisions.

Within Groups and Subsystems

There is increased conformity. Dissenters are shouted down and threatened with expulsion from the subsystem. Pacifism is replaced by competition among leaders and members to assume a position of militant leadership. Group members perceive their group's virtue is preserved by distorting information and coercive decision making. Group members rationalize their philosophy, strategies, tactics, and actions. Between groups and subsystems, the emphasis is on differences rather than similarities. Groups create negative stereotypes of each other. They become blind to their interdependencies. As a consequence, communications and trust decrease and suspicion increases. This combination of elements serves to create self-fulfilling prophecies.

Protective Mechanisms

The focus of attention is on finding someone else or some external event to blame for internal problems encountered when trying to implement the radical change. People are preoccupied with themselves. They detach themselves from others and deny the possibility that they might have contributed to implementation problems. People feel confused in the presence of ambiguity and uncertainty. They doubt themselves and their capacity to cope with the demands of the radical change. They are perplexed and become indecisive.

Problem Solving and Decision Making

These activities become centralized with little, if any, input from below the executive ranks. This centralized authority effectively cuts off leadership from potentially disturbing ground-level realities. Ostensibly, these leadership activities may appear to be based on sound technical and structural considerations, but they are likely to be the result of impulsive hip-shooting that is stimulated by the felt need to do something. Anything. The solutions and decisions may appear to be arbitrary. They may, indeed, be based on leaders' unfounded opinions, beliefs, and wishful thinking. They are aimed at creating quick fixes or tourniquets to stop the bleeding but turn out to be more like leaky Band-Aids.

Policies, Procedures, Rules, and Regulations

During Phase II, these are kept highly traditional. The assumption is that, regardless of radical changes, that which is familiar is safer than trying to adapt and innovate. However, these traditions are often irrelevant and do not serve the changing conditions. Leaders and human resources staff are likely to insist on verbatim compliance to established codes, standards, and criteria. Thus, they enforce rigid adherence to established but anachronistic protocols.

Impacts on Structure

In the absence of decisive and credible leadership, some enterprising employees begin to organize themselves. They experiment and create mechanisms for participatory identification of issues and ways to determine how to solve emerging problems. Informally, they employ what Lewin (in Lewin, 1948) called the *action research method*. That is, with an objective in mind, they take a step that looks promising, assess the results of having taken that step, diagnose the effect and its relation to the objective and then reset or reevaluate their goals and plans, and then they take another action. As some members experiment and innovate, they are likely to involve one another in making joint decisions, planning, acting, and evaluating. As a result of such involvement, they generate commitment among some interdependent parties to support decisions that are made. But these positive activities are not widespread. These innovators are unlikely to achieve much, if any, recognition.

Organizational and Political Barriers

Oshry (2007) pointed out that interface relations between interdependent subsystems tend to deteriorate under conditions that occur during Phase II. Each subsystem seeks to avoid blame for disruptions and discontinuities. Instead, each subsystem, team, and individual seeks scapegoats to blame for their own difficulties. Relations devolve into an “us” versus “them” dynamic. Within subsystems, divisiveness manifests itself in a “top” versus “bottom” dynamic characterized by moderate to high levels of conflict. Under these circumstances, those in the middle feel squeezed by mutually exclusive demands from above and below. Customers, suppliers, and various stakeholder groups (e.g., investors and employee unions) are excluded and are perceived to be external threats to the organization as a whole and to most of its subsystems.

Realistic Leadership

Leaders should make sure that their organizational system or subsystem is thoroughly surveyed. They should scan to gather and then organize relevant information about the effectiveness of leading the radical change as well as any adverse consequences that may have emerged. Leaders should identify sources of and contributions to both effectiveness and adverse consequences. They should also clarify who is affected by the radical change and how these people are reacting, emotionally and behaviorally. Leaders should be aware of and sensitive to the possible range of emotions and behavior during Phase II. A significant percentage of the total population of leaders and members is likely to experience inner turmoil that is characterized by sadness, anxiety, guilt, and rage. They are likely to reminisce and long for their idealized version of the "certainties" that were lost due to the radical change. It is critical that leaders at all levels are empathetic—but definitely not sympathetic. Leaders should honestly declare (as best they can) what will likely be lost, what must be added, and what will stay the same—at least temporarily.

Leaders will have to meet several challenges during Phase II. They should specify the sources, contributions, affected stakeholders, and responses to each emerging risk factor, as well as the opportunities these present. Once committed, leaders must persist and avoid premature termination of the radical change. Also, because some people will attribute significance to marginally important consequences of a radical change, leaders should quickly identify and publicly disconfirm these "superstitious" learnings.

Leaders and their third-party consultants should intervene such that they redirect anger (which is energy) away from self-destructive, ritualistic, or purposeless activities and toward functional, instrumental activities that address the problems created by the radical change. They must repeatedly present a vision of the desired, achievable state. They should regularly convene small groups of representatives of those people who are most affected by the radical change and reinforce the belief that change is possible and desirable. Leaders must regulate and provide focus for identifying and solving implementation problems. They must prevent diversions from solving problems. They must create desirable inducements for achieving the desired state. And they must insist that the human resources functions will continuously update rules, regulations, policies, and procedures as needed. To ensure their effectiveness, leaders and third parties must adopt such attitudes as certainty, unwavering conviction, gentleness, firmness, patience, and persistence.

Phase III: Acknowledgment and Adjustment

Performance and Dissatisfaction

During Phase III, performance drops to the lowest level, and dissatisfaction and frustration rise to the highest level. Self-esteem also drops to its lowest level as people consciously recognize that many of the skill sets that served them well during the pre–radical change have become obsolete. People are quite uncertain if, how, or in what ways they can gain the skills they now need. Many people become fearful that they are superfluous and could lose their jobs. Phase III lasts for weeks for individuals and months for teams, subsystems, and the larger organization.

Leaders and members may not consciously realize that they are confronted by several challenges during Phase III. That is, they have to redefine their desired states—often frequently as conditions change rapidly. They must reframe and specify their present understanding of their current state, in public, to many audiences. They must identify alternative strategies that are likely to enable them to achieve the desired state. However, because their desired states are often a moving target, they must be prepared to generate alternative strategies. Further, they must develop, implement, and monitor the effectiveness of their action plans. This is an implicit action research approach.

Leadership

Leadership during Phase III tends to take the form of "2 × 4" management. That is, "Do what I tell you or I'll hit you over the head with a 2 × 4." Leaders are uncertain, indecisive, and agitated. They become extremely disappointed in those consultants who had predicted a stairstep improvement at this point. Organizational members will struggle to cope with the new demands of the radical change. In addition to their routine activities, they have to take on responsibilities for which they are generally unprepared. This dual set of tasks doubles their normal flow of work and represents overload that results in considerable stress. One can say people are challenged by congestion and compression in dealing with their work and their supply and delivery chains (Freedman, 1997, 2017).

Conflict

There are many signs and symptoms of high levels of conflict during Phase III. For example, there are overt disagreements among various involved parties—often without useful purpose. Some people distort information to gain an advantage over others. Sometimes, people verbally abuse one another. Sabotage to prevent others from gaining an advantage of some sort is not uncommon. Such conflict shows that old, traditional relations between individuals and teams are breaking up.

Emotional Responses

People are likely to experience a variety of emotions. There will be considerable tension among organizational leaders and members, as some are inclined to feel and act impulsively while others are cautious. Some will be suspicious of and doubt the sincerity of others; some may feel cautiously optimistic. Some people will have an emotional investment in and commitment to implementing positive action plans, while others will refrain from making any sort of commitment.

Setting Goals and Planning

These activities are sporadic and tentative in Phase III but can be strengthened by an innovative, explicit action research approach. A few people begin to take a longer time perspective than they did before. They become somewhat aware of systems dynamics and broaden their perspective beyond their immediate concerns.

Protective Mechanisms

A few people will search introspectively for their personal contributions to their problems—that is, their own errors of omission or commission. To protect themselves from excessive anxiety and stress, others are likely to attempt to bargain with leaders and managers to gain security and safety. Even if bargaining is successful, many people will feel depressed because they direct anger at themselves, feeling that they were unable to prevent or successfully cope with the demands of the radical change.

Impacts on Structure

The steeply hierarchical structure that had been in place worked against intergroup cooperation and collaboration but is now, gradually, although in only a few places, replaced with a flatter structure with fewer levels. Thus, during Phase III, in only a few instances, work crosses more easily across lateral and vertical boundaries. Human resources may modify some policies, procedures, rules, and regulations based on input from some relevant involved parties rather than issuing arbitrary mandates. Parts of the organizational system adopt more of an experimental attitude and action research approach. That is, some people become more comfortable with the idea that they can try a new way of doing things for a while and see for themselves what happens. They may then choose to change their desired states and action plans. A few people will adopt an expectation that there will be a continuing stream of shakeouts and modifications in all things. For them, nothing is thought to be written in stone by lightning on top of a mountain. Instead, everything is fluid and malleable. Some people become comfortable with that; others want what they hope for to be written in stone.

Major Consequences

There are at least five notable consequences of Phase III dynamics. First, as previously mentioned, in their anxiety to stop the continuous emergence of unanticipated problems, leaders and managers may resort to a dictatorial, autocratic 2 × 4 managerial style. Second, many of the best and brightest employees who are the most mobile are likely to feel beaten up and leave for safer, more rewarding venues. Third, leaders may prematurely terminate the radical change effort. Fourth, after disappointing leadership by failing to anticipate Phase II and III dynamics and alerting leadership, consultants may be fired (and sued) by those disaffected leaders. Fifth, leaders themselves may leave—voluntarily or otherwise.

Changing Attitudes

Some leaders and members will begin to view other individuals, teams, and subsystems as potentially helpful resources rather than as threats. They become more and more aware of the reality that whatever affects one party has an impact on most others. A few leaders at various levels and some organizational members become increasingly aware of the mutuality of interests among all involved parties. Some leaders and members increasingly share power and influence rather than competing for what had been thought of as a scarce resource. However, these people are likely to be in the minority at this time.

Goal Setting and Planning

In developing action plans, some leaders and managers may begin to collaborate actively with all parties that are likely to be involved in implementation of plans—or that are apt to be impacted by implementation. The input from these stakeholders is likely to be useful in formulating effective action plans. Leaders can focus on coordinating and integrating efforts, especially in achieving multiple objectives simultaneously. They may anticipate the need to make corrective adjustments in plans. They may also participatively develop compatible implementation tactics, methods, and processes. Expert coaching will be needed to guide inexperienced leaders and managers.

Realistic Leadership

To mitigate some problems and prevent others, several interventions by leaders and third-party consultants would be helpful—for example, publicly and repetitively recollecting elements of the past that people thought were lost but will be preserved, clarifying those past elements that are anachronistic and must be let go, envisioning one or more desired states and new elements that must be introduced, and publicly and repetitively pointing to the path or plan between current and desired states. Leaders must make sure that HR staff provides people with opportunities to master new skill sets. It will be essential to prevent precipitous actions and acknowledge and reward persistence. Leaders should also encourage and facilitate exploration, experimentation, and learning from unfolding experience. It will also be necessary to support the self-esteem and dignity of organizational members in all parts and at all levels. Further, leaders must insist, as noted earlier, that human resources staff will continuously update rules, regulations, policies, and procedures as needed.

In general, the purposes of these interventions are to induce a sense of self-discipline in the organization and a commitment among leaders to take responsibility for themselves, their teams, and the entire organization. Leaders should also induce an appreciation and respect for differences and the fundamental, essential interdependency among all parts and levels of the organization. Leaders at all levels should adopt an attitude of reassurance while maintaining persistently high yet achievable expectations. There should be no expressions of sympathy or criticism; to do otherwise will result in people recycling back to the anger they expressed in Phase II.

Leadership style should be flexible because what is required will vary depending on conditions. For example, conditions may remain steady at either a high or low level of pressure and complexity. From time to time, conditions will become quite volatile and shift from low to high pressure and complexity when a crisis or emergency arises. In any event, it would be a major error to assume that a single leadership style will serve adequately under any and all internal and external conditions.

Phase IV: Adaptation and Change or Reconstruction

Time Span and Nature of Impact

This phase generally covers a period of months for individuals and years for the total organization. During this time, performance and self-esteem will gradually rise, while frustration and dissatisfaction will diminish as people increasingly learn how to cope with the demands of the radical change (Freedman, 2017).

Emotions

People begin to feel hopeful. As they see that they are learning to cope, they feel increasingly optimistic and take pride in their accomplishments.

They feel increasingly committed to making sure the action plans are implemented. Many people will feel cautious and reserve judgment and remain patiently on the sidelines. People will feel an increasing sense of pride and self-esteem as they see themselves becoming increasingly competent in coping with the consequences of the radical change. Their regard for the contributions of others will also increase.

Perspective

People begin to extend their time perspective during Phase IV. They focus on the recent past as well as the near term and, increasingly, the near- and long-term future. Their focus of attention also shifts. People increasingly let go of anachronistic attachments, with respect and appreciation for their historic contributions. They identify and preserve functional attachments to new, internal sources of safety and security. They also attach to new, added on (or revitalized) sources of safety and security. Expert coaches and leaders can help people make these shifts explicit so that they acknowledge and take pride in their accomplishments.

Problem Solving and Decision Making

These processes should evolve and become both functional and flexible (Ruma, 1974). The critical questions are "Does the chosen decision or action serve a useful purpose?" and "Can we, or are we willing, to change the decision?"

Realistic Leadership

Leaders should employ a data-based diagnostic approach to ensure that adequate resources are matched to prioritized tasks, activities, and functions. Again, expert coaching will probably be needed to ensure that leaders approach problems and decisions in a comprehensive, effective manner.

Thinking Processes

These also evolve. People increasingly identify issues based on what is likely to contribute to or obstruct the achievement of results. People also make increasingly realistic decisions based on a systemic, holistic perspective with broad time horizons. Expert coaches can assist leadership to make these processes conscious so they can better control and evaluate them.

Impacts on Structure

System structure follows an evolutionary trend toward lateral business processes to a greater extent than vertical functional hierarchies. Expert coaches can help leadership to clarify and validate this trend.

Interface relationships between teams and subsystems gradually become characterized by mutual understanding, appreciation, and acceptance of the essential uniqueness and interdependence of work units. There will be more respectful cooperation. Work units will take differentiated but integrated action. Communications will become less guarded and more authentic, timely, and proactive. Expert coaching will probably be useful.

Goal Setting and Planning

In setting goals during Phase IV, leaders at all levels should examine and select among alternative strategic goals as well as tactical objectives and the plans needed to achieve them. They should repetitively communicate those goals, objectives, and plans with all significantly involved work units and obtain their feedback—whether that feedback is critical or confirmatory. They may modify their goals, objectives, and plans to accommodate any divergent needs of the involved parties based, in part, on the feedback they receive.

Policies, Procedures, Rules, and Regulations

These become increasingly living documents. They are changeable based on input and feedback from all involved parties about emerging, changing conditions. These documents must be oriented toward achieving the shared, common, established strategic direction. Coaches can remind leaders that life is a series of temporary realities. There is no stable steady state.

Realistic Leadership

Leaders at all levels should strive to publicly demonstrate how their tactical objectives contribute to the achievement of the strategic goals and how the strategic goals support and align with the organization's mission and values. They must also make sure the tactical objectives and strategic goals are assigned to the most appropriate work units. However, although these are functions that leaders and managers should perform, many are unlikely to realize that these functions are their responsibility, nor are they likely to have the skills needed to execute them. Expert consulting and coaching will be necessary.

There are many tasks that leaders at all levels and in all parts of the organization should perform during Phase IV. For example, they should create and preserve the cohesiveness of their various intact work units. They should encourage intergroup cooperation and coordinate activities across subsystems. They should closely observe the implementation of action plans and gather and test the significance of data about the impacts of the execution of these action plans. People should pay close attention to possible side effects and unintended consequences; they will have to identify and deal with these as well as previously dormant issues that become evident as action plans are implemented. Ideally, people should also archive, organize, and disseminate lessons learned. Just because these tasks should be performed does not mean they will be. Existing leadership is unlikely to know that they should make sure these tasks are performed, so it is essential to have knowledgeable, experienced expert consultants available to coach leaders.

There are two primary purposes of leaders and third-party consultants during Phase IV. These are, first, to institutionalize or lock in, reinforce, and applaud the functional achievements of leaders and managers and their subordinates. Second, they must prevent complacency, which is likely if people think of their current achievements as having completely realized the desired state. There is still a lot of work to be done. So, leaders and third parties must maintain vigilance and provide continuous support for emerging results. The procedures that have been invented to effectively analyze problems and develop solutions must be institutionalized.

Relaxation is important but must be regulated. Achievements should be celebrated while people learn from failures. These lessons learned should be institutionalized. The internal and external organizational environments should be scanned constantly in a search for new, emerging problems. Leadership should insist, once again, that human resources continuously update rules, regulations, policies, and procedures as needed. Expert consultants will probably be needed to coach leaders and managers in performing these functions as they are often neglected.

Leaders' Attitude

Leaders and managers should adopt an attitude characterized by active friendliness, approval of positive actions, and humility about their own contributions, and they should express pride in, and appreciative approval for, lower-level leaders, managers, individual contributors, and interface coordinators. Leaders should discourage inappropriate attitudes or expectations about the third-party consultants; no idealization of or dependency on the third parties should exist. People need to feel that they have achieved their results on their own.

Perhaps the most important support that leadership can provide is empathy. Leaders should express understanding and appreciation of the legitimacy of the feelings that people are likely to experience throughout the process of dealing with the challenges of radical change. That is, people will benefit from their leaders' heartfelt expression of their belief that the anxiety, fear, and anger that people experience, particularly during Phases I, II, and III, are normal responses to crazy, unprecedented situations. They are not at all crazy responses to normal circumstances.

In summary, leaders and their third-party consultants should take all four phases into account when they formulate their strategic and tactical plans for leading and managing radical changes. In the absence of focused consideration of these highly probable dynamics, planning is likely to be based on wishes and hopes. This will lead to frustration and disappointment, not to mention a considerable waste of time and energy. The four phases of leading and managing radical change are presented in Figure 4.3 in a diagrammatical form.

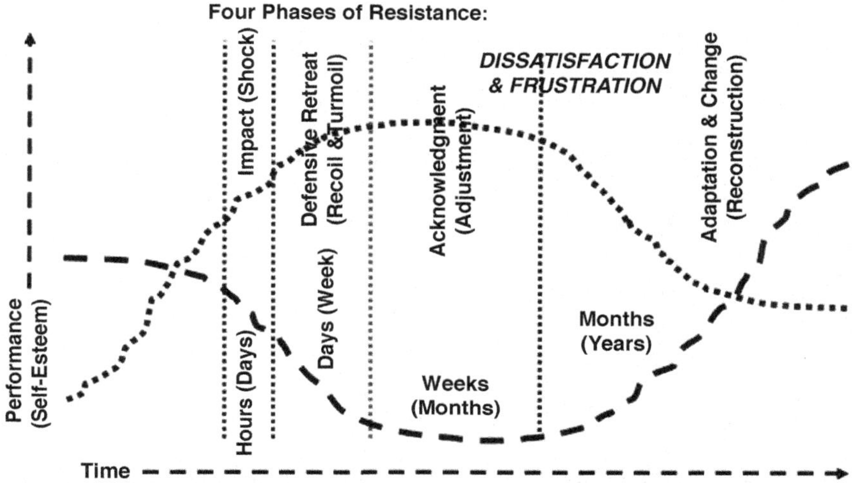

Figure 4.3

Note. The realistic model of leading radical change. Adapted from *Leading Radical Change in Complex Organizations: A Field Book* (p. 160), by A. M. Freedman, 2017, ClearSpace. Copyright 2017 by ClearSpace. Adapted with permission.

IMPLICATIONS FOR CONSULTING PSYCHOLOGISTS

The models described in this chapter—the Phoenix and Swamp models, complex systems change strategies, and phases of change—can be usefully applied to understand radical organizational change. This chapter also provides an understanding of radical change from a phenomenological standpoint—the look and feel of change on the inside of organizations for employees as well as leadership.

The idealistic Phoenix organizational change model, in the main, is unrealistic; it is too simplistic and assumes that all of the elements of the organization described in the Swamp model will work without friction to move seamlessly through the various stages of organizational change. Attention to the organizational processes described in the Swamp model as well as the more predictable and likely phases of change described in this chapter will prepare leadership for the most likely reactions and responses to planned interventions.

With effective leadership and management throughout the four phases, leaders, organizational members, as well as internal and external stakeholders can realistically expect some particularly positive results. Particularly in Phases I and II, there will be less performance deterioration compared with unmanaged radical change. There will be an enhanced understanding of and tolerance for the expression of emotions such as frustration and dissatisfaction. There will be minimal loss of essential personnel. There will be a considerable reduction in lowered performance. There will be a faster recovery. Performance and self-esteem are both likely to exceed the original expectations that are presented in the reasonable but unrealistic Phoenix model.

5

Covert Processes in Human Affairs

This chapter discusses and demonstrates how consultants can use knowledge of psychodynamics and covert processes in their consulting and coaching practices.

THE CASE OF INCOMPREHENSIBLE INDISCRETION

"I have something I need to talk to you about today," said Marty Mariano, the senior vice president (SVP) of one of the largest strategic business units in a medium-sized consumer services company.[1] Marty had been in his position for more than 3 years and had done an excellent job of assuming command, reconfiguring his leadership team, and advancing the performance of the organization on virtually every measurable metric. Tall, handsome, self-assured, and dressed in the business-casual slacks, shirt,

[1] This case is fictional.

https://doi.org/10.1037/0000328-005
Essential Strategies for Organizational and Systems Change: An Overview for Consultants, by H. S. Leonard, R. R. Kilburg, and A. M. Freedman

and blazer typical of the company's culture, he was always the picture of a well-put-together leader.

"What do you have on your mind?" I[2] asked.

"It's hard to put into words, but with a couple of my direct reports, I've recently found myself saying more to them about what is happening in the company, that upon reflection, is probably not very wise."

"Can you give me an example?"

"I've shared confidences with them about what has been happening at the senior leadership level. If anyone there discovered what I've said, I could be in trouble for violating expectations concerning confidential discussions," he said, looking at his hands folded on the table between us.

"Are the risks serious?"

"Well, I don't really know. I trust my people, and I've made it clear that the information is not to be shared. But . . ."

"But you never know?" I finished his sentence.

Marty nodded his head and sighed.

We had worked together for nearly the entire time since his promotion. He had hired me on the recommendation of several other former clients of mine. The initial agreement was to support him during the opening phase of his succession as the SVP. The engagement had morphed over time to one comprising a number of other aspects of his and his organization's performance. I had found Marty to be conscientious, quick to act on most of the issues we discussed, and courageous in making difficult choices and acting on them with speed, integrity, and a strong sense of personal and business ethics. He was in every way a model client.

"What's your take on what's going on?" I prodded.

Marty sighed again. "I'm not sure. I don't think these disclosures are necessary for business reasons. About the only thing I've been able to come up with on my own is that I felt some kind of need to please these folks."

"Have you ever had this experience before?"

Marty smiled quickly, and then it extinguished like a match gone cold in the wind.

[2] Throughout this chapter, first-person statements refer to the observations and experiences of Richard Kilburg, the second author of this book.

"I think I do it all the time, but these were somehow more noticeable."

What ensued was more than an hour of very intense discussion of several historical examples of his ingratiation propensities; his roles in his family of origin; and his relationships with his father as "the golden child" and with his mother, who was "never satisfied with anything I did." Tears rolled down his cheeks when he talked about both of his parents, particularly his father, whom he lost the year before. A complex pattern of adaptive behavior that largely had served him well in his life and career to that point revealed itself well beyond anything we had explored previously. To summarize the complex work Marty had done in that session, I asked, "Would you like an idea or two about what we have just explored?"

"Please," Marty replied.

"From the data and stories you have just provided both of us, we appear to have uncovered some very significant threads that tie this together for us. As an accomplished and polished extravert, you seem to have continuously experienced almost a compulsive need to ingratiate yourself with and prove yourself to everyone in your life. Despite checking every achievement box in sight, you have experienced a kind of nagging doubt about yourself and your performance. Even when you are doing very well and hearing positive feedback, you expect to be intensively criticized in hurtful and unpredictable ways. Does that sound accurate to you?" Nearing the end of our session, he smiled at me, nodded, and said, "Well, at least now I know why I've been doing this crap. Now, all I need to do is stop it."

PSYCHODYNAMICS AND THE CENTRALITY OF PATTERN RECOGNITION IN CONSULTING ON CHANGE

This very succinct case report demonstrates the importance and validity of psychodynamic expertise in the practice of consultation. A seemingly superior professional in the middle of climbing to the top of an organizational leadership pyramid and in every measurable way performing in truly spectacular fashion nevertheless engages in a lifelong pattern of extraverted ingratiation and self-promotion that consciously, he absolutely knows is not only wrong at an operational level, it also threatens virtually everything that he and his colleagues in management have worked toward for a long time. It was not just the disclosures themselves that were dangerous. The fact that as a very trusted, fast-tracked insider he would violate key norms for communication of the senior leadership team threatened to undermine many of the aspects of that group's structures and processes. The discovery of such leakage would no doubt produce conflict and consternation in the executive group. And as is always the case with even the best of senior teams, their relationships, group dynamics, and overall performance together were metastable and dependent on a wide variety of both overt and covert processes. As most consultants and leaders know, violations of trust can occur in an instant of thoughtless behavior and, depending on the maturity and depth of investment in and between those leaders, at times are nearly impossible to mend.

Consultants must be constantly aware of the unseen, unheard, and covertly expressed aspects of human behavior in their engagements. As the work of organizational change has become more sophisticated, data driven, and reliant on goal-congruent and behaviorally specific planning and implementation efforts, it can be difficult to identify such covert structures and processes yet alone to know how to intervene when they are identified (Kilburg, 2000; Marshak, 2006; Oshry, 2007). This chapter is designed to introduce key concepts and skills that can be used to improve consultants' abilities to perform in addressing these challenging and nebulous matters of individual, group, organizational, and large systems behavior.

The history of science is based on the efforts of millions and millions of humans acting individually or in concert to discover the patterns that drive the natural world in which they did and do live. The discernment and illumination of these patterns have yielded amazing insights and ever more complex and useful technologies that support continued human progress.

Included in these studies have been consistent efforts to understand what makes for effective human organization and performance. These initiatives reached a significant apex in the middle of the 20th century with the creation of general systems theory (von Bertalanffy, 1969). Started in the 1930s, von Bertalanffy's efforts were designed initially to determine what structures and processes were held in common by all living creatures. The publication of his ideas after World War II coincided with the rise of information theory and cybernetics, and they quickly merged into a powerful set of concepts and tools for the exploration of patterns of organization in virtually every field of study. Chapter 4 provides a succinct summary of many of the variants in the approaches to illuminate and apply general systems theory to human activity, especially in organizations. As noted in that chapter, the contributions of A. Kuhn (1972) and A. Kuhn and Beam (1982) were extensive and remain very useful to consultants in their efforts to discover the most meaningful and relevant patterns of behavior in the performance of any organization.

The vast majority of enterprises that consultants serve are controlled, acting systems in Kuhn's terminology. They have structures, processes, and contents that are specific to their designed and explicitly defined purposes. They pursue actively either states of sustained productive equilibrium or periods of growth and development while simultaneously working to avoid regressive slides into maladaptation. Kilburg et al. (1998) used these concepts to present a model of organizational performance that posited five major stages on a continuum of enterprise development from super-resilience on the positive side to decay and death on the other.

In Kuhn's approaches, organizations that struggle or fail to identify goals, move progressively to attain them, and have difficulty maintaining any specific equilibria or pursuing growth are likely to demonstrate moves away from being controlled, acting systems and toward performing as pattern systems that have elements that may be defined and interact but do not have orchestrated goals and sustained, well-managed relationships among detector, selector, and effector structures and processes. The organization of these institutions from elements to subsystems, to systems and supersystems, becomes more chaotic and dysfunctional over time. And unless specific interventions are made to change these states, real trouble inevitably leads to failure and dismemberment. Systems perspectives like those of Kuhn can, do, and should guide any consultant on where to look and what to seek in their efforts to uncover the most relevant patterns in any client engagement (Cummings & Worley, 2015; Gharajedaghi, 2011).

These approaches to the study and management of organizations offer leaders and consultants a virtual cornucopia of ideas, methods, and models for creating, assessing, and changing enterprises. Most of the time, they provide either general or specific descriptions of the elements of systems, the ways in which they interact, the outcomes they produce, and, therefore, how they can be directed and modified. The essence of modern administrative approaches is to collect data on these systemic components of organizational operations that then enable leaders to engage rational choice making on a moment-to-moment or longer-term strategic basis. However, as described in the case study opening this chapter, some systems of behavior that significantly influence individuals, groups, and institutions are not readily observable, nor are they measurable in most direct ways. These patterns have been given many different names—covert, unconscious, or psychodynamic (Czander, 1993; Diamond, 1993; Kets de Vries, 2006; Kilburg, 2000; Levinson, 2002; Marshak, 2006), but within Kuhn's terminology, they are all acting systems. With careful examination, their goals and the types of outcomes they are intended to produce—growth, equilibrium, or regression and decay can be identified and used as part of any consulting or coaching engagement.

Psychodynamics has been defined as follows:

> the systematized knowledge and theory of human behavior and its motivation, the study of which depends largely upon the functional significance of emotion. Psychodynamics recognizes the role of unconscious motivation in human behavior. The science of psychodynamics assumes that one's behavior is determined by past experience, genetic endowment, and current reality. (American Psychiatric Association, 1980, p. 112)

More recently, in the introduction to the second edition of the *Psychodynamic Diagnostic Manual* (PDM-2), Lingiardi and McWilliams (2017) noted the following:

> PDM-2 adds a needed perspective on symptom patterns depicted in existing taxonomies, enabling clinicians to describe and categorize personality patterns, related social and emotional capacities, unique mental profiles, and personal experiences of symptoms. In focusing on the full range of mental functioning, PDM-2 aspires to be a "taxonomy of people" rather than a "taxonomy of disorders." (p. 2)

This massive reference work stretches more than 1,000 pages and demonstrates just how far the study and application of psychodynamic patterns have progressed, at least for their use in assessing and intervening in problems involving individual behavior.

ESSENTIAL PSYCHODYNAMIC MODELS

Although most assuredly well known for its contributions to the understanding and treatment of mental and nervous disorders, for well over a century, psychodynamic inquiries and concepts have been broadly and successfully applied to help understand and intervene in the behavior of families, groups, organizations, and large social systems. Kilburg (1995) provided a complex and integrated model of psychodynamics and systems theory for use in organization development interventions. After this, Kilburg (2000, 2004) succinctly reviewed the scientific support for psychodynamic concepts while applying them to coaching executives. Carr and Gabriel (2001) briefly summarized the general background and types of contributions to the management of organizational change for which psychodynamic theory and methods are used. Thus, for the interested and motivated leader or consultant, there are a wide variety of resources available to explore these issues in more depth than can be accomplished in this chapter.

One of the most fundamental issues for any consultant working with individuals, groups, organizations, and large social systems is how they come to understand the purposes, structures, processes, history, and deeply ingrained habits that comprise their behaviors. Finding meaning in these patterns (Levinson, 2002; Weick, 1995, 2001) leads invariably to diagnostic impressions and the formulation of intervention plans used to guide the management of change.

The 17-dimensional model of psychodynamics and systems elements introduced by Kilburg (1995) comprises 11 psychodynamic components and the six principle system concepts routinely found in most texts on that subject. Either implicitly at the beginning of my work in leadership and consulting or more formally for the past 25 years, this model operates intuitively for me as I work in organizations. As the model depicts, these 17 dimensions are routinely experienced by consultants in their work with the behaviors of individuals, groups, work units and subunits, or an entire organization.

For all of their usefulness and importance, psychodynamic approaches to understanding leadership and various other aspects of organizational performance are rarely taught in formal training programs for managers or consultants. In my work with clients and organizations over a 50-year period, I can personally attest to the absence of this type of expertise in leaders and in most consultants.

Historically speaking, there are two major anchors in psychodynamic theory. First is *conflict theory*, developed by Sigmund Freud and his colleagues in the Vienna Circle (Kilburg, 2004, 2020). The length of this chapter makes any reasonable delineation of this approach impossible to provide. That said, Freud advocated that every human starts their journey in life in an undifferentiated state of primary narcissism. In essence, initially, there is little overt evidence of the full adult presence of the unique human that eventually develops over time in the newborn infant. All human babies are primarily motivated to survive and meet their primary needs for security. They express themselves in the most direct, earnest, and often caustic fashion. Freud labeled the first identifiable internal mental and emotional structure that is completely self-absorbed the *id*. It operates according to the Pleasure Principle. What it wants, it strives to get no matter what constraints are encountered. In doing so, infants establish relationships with caretakers, most of whom are more or less able to help babies survive. In due time, caretakers put overt and covert pressure on infants to change their behavior to conform to the demands of the external world.

Over several years, this fluid and challenging set of interactions puts enormous stress on every child. The child's instinctual needs must be harmonized or at least compromised with these external edicts. As this unfolds, infants' mental and emotional structures and processes evolve, and they rapidly begin to understand that there are other humans upon whom their well-being, pleasure, and survival depend. The *ego* or rational self within a child thus grows rapidly in this interactive environment, differentiates from the id, and learns that to survive and continue to grow, it must operate according to the reality principle (Freud, 1923/1971). As difficult as the process is to master, the child must be able to negotiate and compromise with other people. At a very young age, children also begin to learn the difference between right and wrong (Piaget, 1965). Freud (1930/2005) argued that the ability to mentally and emotionally make these distinctions forces a further differentiation of the ego into what he called the *superego*. It operates by the moral principle, primarily using an internalized sense of guilt to influence both the id and the ego to do what it perceives as correct—namely, moral acts and thoughts. The superego and the ego are enabled by another structure called the *ego ideal*, which also emerges over time and comprises goals, images, biases, and perceptions of what constitutes exceptional behavior and performance for an individual.

The essence of psychodynamic conflict theory argues that the needs and other forms of motivations of any human arise in interactions with the external world and as a result of their own drives, emotions, thoughts, values, beliefs, habits, and so on. The individual person is faced constantly with demands to meet the desires for immediate pleasure expressed by the id/instinctual self, the requirements to compromise with the forces and constraints of reality required by the ego/rational self, and the precepts and commands of the superego/conscience as filtered through the elements of the ideal self to do what it always perceives as right and righteous and providing more pleasure than pain. Personality, conflict structures, competencies, mental illness, and personal and professional performance and expertise evolve out of this constant churning cauldron of conflict. The results of these perennial conflicts are what Freud labeled as *compromise formations*. These complex patterns of thoughts, feelings, sensations, perceptions, and overt and covert forms of behavior are what every leader and consultant must strive to be aware of in themselves, their colleagues, and their adversaries, and in the structures and processes within which they work.

Wurmser (2007) identified six major subtypes of psychodynamic conflict with which consultants should become familiar:

- emotions and their management
- the desire to see and operate in the world clearly and creatively using curiosity

- basic identity issues
- control over oneself and one's environment
- competition and triangular relationships
- complexities involved in questions and issues involving loyalty

Any one or all of these domains of conflict can be operating in any given set of circumstances within an individual or between groups of people. Again, our opening case example illustrates a long-standing set of internal conflicts operating inside of Marty and comprising elements of his relationships with his parents that then manifested themselves in his working relationships, directly and overtly with some of his subordinates, and unconsciously with his peers and superiors.

The second major theoretical arm of psychodynamics is *object relations theory*. Initially, this approach evolved out of the work of Melanie Klein and a small group of her colleagues (Klein, 1975a, 1975b; Klein & Riviere, 1964). While agreeing with the classic conflict theory that the human infant begins in a state of largely undifferentiated narcissism, they emphasized the centrality of the intimate and complex relationship formed between the baby and its primary caretaker—most often, the mother. In this theoretical perspective, the child quickly recognizes its state of primal dependency on that caretaker, symbolized by the nourishing breast. Equally quickly, the infant grasps that the breast/caretaker is not under its control. The existential threat and displeasure experienced by the repeated and sudden disappearance and equally magical reappearance of the all-nourishing and nurturing mother/parent leads the child to experience a continual state of envy (Kilburg, 2020; Klein, 1975a, 1975b), along with its associated primary negative emotions of rage, shame, anxiety, and sadness. Over the first months and years of life, all humans are subject to these forces, and as a result of the sustained stresses and strains they must endure, every person begins to form essential patterns of relationships that come to influence, if not dominate, the rest of their lives. Over a number of decades, object relations theorists have come to call these patterns *attachment styles* (Ainsworth, 1969; Ainsworth et al., 1978; Bowlby, 1988). The five primary styles are

1. secure–approaching and supporting
2. insecure–tenuous

3. insecure–avoidant
4. insecure–ambivalent
5. insecure–disorganized

Succinct descriptions of each of these patterns of human relatedness are provided in Kilburg (2004).

Following the theoretical foundations of object relations theory obviously leads consultants and leaders to direct their attention to the functional and dysfunctional aspects of the relationships of those involved in and with any organization. What one hopes for, tries to identify, and continuously tries to develop are the patterns of secure relatedness that knit together high-functioning teams, groups, units, and whole organizations and that enable superior performance. It is usually the securely attached individuals one encounters who provide the greatest potential for development and change in any consulting engagement. Unfortunately, even in the best of circumstances, most organizations are composed of individuals with widely varying attachment styles. And as described above, initially, these patterns are largely invisible and operate covertly within individuals and between dyads, triads, and other types of groups. As in our opening case study, discovering and uncovering the structures, processes, history, thoughts, feelings, behaviors, and people that drive the deployment of these styles can take a very long time and require a sustained and highly trusting relationship between consultants and their clients. In other situations, the attachment style of an individual leader, consultant, group, or even organization can be fairly easily identified even if it remains difficult to engage.

Traditionally, inside of psychoanalytic/psychodynamic theory and practice, these complex patterns of conflict between the inner and outer worlds of people and their approaches to the relationships in which they operate were discerned in the context of a healing endeavor pursued by a patient/client and a therapist (Brenner, 1976, 1982). Freud's lifetime of intellectual and clinical work that produced a great deal of the early formulations of psychodynamic theory was pursued with the main goal of understanding what produced mental illness and complex, biologically inexplicable forms of human suffering. The means to the end of misery was the development of a special type of relationship called *transference*, in and through which the client came to enact parts of or the entire pattern that they had cocreated with others to manage the complexities of their life (Freud, 1912/1964; Racker, 1968) with the therapist. The emergence of the transference, its recognition and assessment by the therapist, and the interpretation of its impact on the client formed the essential elements of the process. As more and more experience was gained in working with and through transference relationships, it became clear that the interpretations of the therapist, no matter how accurate and well delivered, were in and of themselves necessary but insufficient to achieve change and relief of a patient's suffering. Over the long run, clients had to move from simple recognition of inappropriate and destructive patterns of thoughts, feelings, and behavior to change what are in essence very, very deeply conditioned habits by deconditioning and then reconditioning them into more constructive and creative patterns in and through which to live (Wood & Rünger, 2016).

In the late 20th and early 21st centuries, these two elemental approaches were challenged by and integrated into a revised model of psychodynamic understanding and intervention. This set of concepts has been loosely labeled as *intersubjectivity theory*. Without delving deeply into this approach, the essential recognition was that the transference relationship was not composed solely of the patterns and reactions of a client to their past events, situations, and specific relationships and then displaced onto the therapist with whom they were working. Rather, what slowly unfolded in the therapeutic work was a deeper comprehension of what is called the *countertransference relationship*: the complex set of reactions set off in a therapist by the interaction they have with the client through the entire course of working with them (Christian, 2015; Langs, 1976; Masterson, 1983). Intersubjectivity theory, with its increased emphasis on a careful examination of the contributions of both therapist and client to the relationship they experience and mutually produce, points to the need for ever deepening and more nuanced comprehension of what takes place between two or more individuals. Benjamin (2011) and others have described how challenging this can be even when a therapist is well versed and trained to look for these phenomena in a working relationship with a client.

Although a substantial number of psychologists and other consultants have had the benefit of extensive education and training in psychodynamic theory, in my experience, they constitute a small minority of the professionals working in change management in organizations. A deep comprehension of implicit and explicit conflicts, approaches to relationship formation and enactment, and the complexities of how consultants and clients interact with each other is incomparably useful in the conduct of any engagement. These issues are often the most definitively challenging for consultants and clients alike. When they arise and are not addressed, they can often completely derail what might otherwise be a superbly designed and executed change project.

WHEN TO USE PSYCHODYNAMIC APPROACHES IN CONSULTATION

In one sense, once a professional change agent becomes familiar or intimate with psychodynamics, the ideas and methods involved are never completely out of their awareness. Virtually every form of data produced by an individual, group, or organization can be examined from these perspectives. In reality, however, as useful as these approaches can be, in the majority of consulting situations, they are best kept as the personal observations and reactions of the practitioner. Unnecessary and untimely use of these kinds of ideas and interventions can also seriously derail an engagement. For example, what we could describe as usual and customary conversations about the financial performance of an enterprise do not often lend themselves to a deep dive into the personal histories or relationship dynamics of a leader or a leadership team. Among a long list of potential domains in which to use these approaches, Kilburg (2004) suggested that consultants should consider them when self-awareness, family, group, and organizational awareness and savvy; emotional containment and management; executive performance; behavioral flexibility and creativity; human resiliency; and interpersonal, group, and intra-/interorganizational conflict are present in an engagement.

In that same paper, Kilburg (2004) suggested a large set of circumstances in which psychodynamic approaches might be usefully deployed.

These include situations in which an individual, group, organizational unit, or entire enterprise continues to misbehave or underperform despite the consciously stated intention and desire to improve and do well; suffers from powerful disorganizing and disruptive emotional experiences and reactions for which there are no obvious explanations; or faces repeated situations and problems in families, groups, and organizations that are incomprehensible and destructive and for which there are no obvious answers or previous intervention efforts have failed.

As can be seen from these examples, the range of issues, challenges, and problems for which psychodynamic sensitivities and competencies might be applicable is extensive. However, it is extremely important for any consultant to exercise exquisite judgment in making determinations to intervene with these approaches. Unless an individual client or client organization has been appropriately prepared to expect that the consultant may well raise such issues or considerations, it is almost axiomatic that strong emotional reactions and defensive operations will be forthcoming. When consultants are unprepared for such responses, severe damage to a change project and even to the working relationship between them and the primary client can occur. In several situations with which I have been familiar, I have also witnessed a consultant being discharged from engagements and contracts and even long-standing agreements being terminated. So caution is always warranted before proceeding rapidly or in depth with this kind of material.

ESSENTIAL ELEMENTS OF PSYCHODYNAMICALLY INFORMED CONSULTING INTERVENTIONS

Once consultants have collected sufficient information to convince themselves that covert, unconscious patterns of behavior are interfering with the productive performance of an individual, group, or organizational client and that it would be useful, even necessary, to bring this to conscious awareness and thus to the work of change, they are faced with the conundrum of how best to do this in a way that advances and improves the consultation and does not produce unnecessary pain and defensive reactions. Defensive reactions automatically lead to resistance to change, and they can be extensive, complex, and wonderfully creative (Kilburg, 2000). Despite these complexities and potential dangers, consultants must proceed with caution, courage, and wisdom to address what has been discerned as substantial trouble.

Bringing together the material that has been collected in a way that a client can comprehend and begin to contemplate actively is an art, not a science. The essence of it involves creating an *interpretation*, or accurate picture of what appears to be the pattern that causes the difficulty. The introductory case study presents a succinct version of what an interpretation can involve. Nearing the end of the working session with Marty, who had produced a great deal of meaningful and deeply emotional material, I knew I needed to pull several major strands of the data together so he could understand for himself how major aspects of the pattern cohered and powered the behavior that he found so troubling. I tried to integrate aspects of his personality, approaches to performance, achievements, deeply troubling emotions, and key aspects of his complex historical relationships with his now deceased parents. His reaction to the way in which I was able to frame the observations suggested strongly that he understood and was able to, at least temporarily, see the pattern and its influence in his executive life. Such open and receptive responses constitute behavioral confirmation that the interpretation was decently constructed and has made sense to or been partially accepted by a client. The reverse is equally true. Denial of the validity of an interpretation, strong negative emotional reactions, and vocal arguments about the accuracy of all or part of what is presented are all evidence that even if the intervention was appropriate in its content, timing, structure, and manner of delivery, the client may not be ready, willing, or able to engage the material presented at that time.

Most often in consulting work, the necessity to intervene with such an "interpretation" evolves over time as information is forthcoming from a variety of sources. However, the timing and construction of what is to be said often emerges quite spontaneously and unpredictably. In the moment, this creates a pretty consistent experience for the consultant of crawling out on a limb of a tree that may actually feel quite unsubstantial when the timing becomes intuitively obvious and necessary. Often, the recognition of a pattern involves the exercise of professional intuition in ways that can be disconcerting to both the client and the consultant (Kilburg, 2006). When timed well and framed meaningfully, progress is often made in the change project. However, a poorly timed, framed, or delivered interpretation can significantly inhibit movement forward. Kilburg (2004, p. 263) provided a succinct summary of the characteristics of an effective behavioral or psychodynamically informed intervention in executive coaching engagements. These characteristics are equally applicable to work on covert, unconscious material with groups and organizations.

As discussed earlier, virtually nothing happens in any organization unless it is mediated by and through one or more relationships, the second major element in these types of interventions. In coaching and consulting work on change management, this is also the case. However, there are several major differences in the structure of relationships between consultants/coaches and their clients as opposed to those between leaders and their subordinates, peers, and superiors. To be sure, the client exercises authority over the consultant or coach in the construction of an agreement, in evaluating the success or failure of any change initiative, and in determining the effectiveness of the performance of the professional who has been hired. However, feedback between coaches or consultants and their clients is multidimensional, nearly constant, and by design and in operation not hierarchically determined. Although work can and is directly delegated by leaders to their coaches and consultants, the reverse is equally true when a coach/consultant requests the client(s) to perform various tasks, collect and report data, and often to do homework assignments. These relationships are simultaneously fluid and structured, and the boundaries are often much more permeable than other types of working relationships. However, when working on psychodynamically informed issues, consultants and coaches are wise to keep in mind a number of the components of "complementarity" inherent in an intimate working relationship suggested by Wurmser (2007).

The nature of the working relationship between any coach or consultant and their client is indeed complex and challenging. Most often, a change management engagement does not make any effort either to identify or to specify any of the intimate features of how the individuals involved will behave toward, react to, or coconstruct expectations of those people who participate. If described at all, a list of "deliverables" most often is written into the agreement between the parties. These usually describe work products, their contents, and the timeframes within which they will be produced. The relationship work itself or how the work will be done by the people involved in any project is more or less assumed and most often only addressed if and when problems arise. However, anyone with any experience in providing consulting services knows both explicitly and implicitly that these relationship issues often determine whether any effort will succeed or fail.

A third major element in a psychodynamically informed intervention addresses what remains as the most significant and challenging problem in the management of change, intervention adherence. A wide variety of books and papers have been produced over many decades that focus on why efforts at changing aspects of human behavior fail. Pasmore (2011) suggested that up to 75% of change management initiatives do not meet their objectives. Any number of issues has been identified as contributing to this problem, including lack of trust, cynicism toward change initiatives, resistances of varying types, lack of change readiness work, and organizational culture. Yet, often overlooked in these extensive examinations are the fundamentals of learning and habit formation.

Wood and Rünger (2016), cited earlier, in their extensive review of habit formation and its associated challenges, reaffirmed that the scientific foundations supporting the fundamental aspects of learning remain unchallenged. The three main forms of conditioning a new behavior have been known and well understood for decades and include *classical conditioning*, often called associative learning; *operant conditioning*, often called contingency learning; and *social learning* involving social modeling or observation. Leonard (2002) provided virtually a condensed and encyclopedic summary of theoretical approaches to learning.

Inherent in all these approaches and fundamental to all efforts to learn are the time and energy required, the difficulties in retaining a newly acquired behavior, the strength of habits long practiced and deeply rewarded, the challenges of unlearning something once gained, and the likelihood that old patterns of performance, no matter how deeply de- or reconditioned, can reemerge rapidly—indeed, automatically—if the conditions are right. This latter process is called *spontaneous recovery.* Thus, the matter of what it takes to maintain new learning assumes an important if misunderstood and underappreciated aspect of any change management project. This includes any initiative to utilize psychodynamic theory or methods to induce a redirection in motivation or action.

Finally, several significant problems often lead to failure and non-adherence to changes after they are made. These can include insufficient agreement or goal clarity; a lack of explicit commitment to development by either the client(s) or consultant(s), often experienced as a lack of follow-through or necessary practice on the part of clients; insufficient competence in either the client(s) or the consultant(s); excessive defensiveness, conflicts, or negative emotionality; and regression in either the client(s') or consultant(s') organization. These problems can arise either acutely and spontaneously at any point in conducting a change initiative, or they can operate chronically and out of the conscious awareness of the people involved. These challenges routinely come to light when a change process stalls or fails altogether and the need for either a formal or informal assessment of the difficulties arises. At times, an assessment can lead to changes in the structures, processes, or contents of the project; at other times, an assessment can clarify that the effort, however well intended, was actually doomed because of one or more of the issues highlighted in this chapter.

IMPLICATIONS OF USING A PSYCHODYNAMIC APPROACH FOR CONSULTING PSYCHOLOGISTS

The concepts and the case material presented here demonstrate that the study and use of psychodynamically informed ideas and methods in consulting work can be important and effective for virtually any practitioner. The historic theoretical approaches as well as initial scientific observations and cases illuminating psychodynamics are now well over 100 years old. Yet we hope this chapter has opened readers' eyes and increased their curiosity about how to learn more and develop additional expertise in this arena for themselves to use in the 21st century. The materials presented are foundational, historically anchored, and simultaneously informed—and, ideally, invigorated—by contemporary case material. Whether we are attuned to it or not, unconscious, covert motivation and behavior surrounds and engages all of us every day. The empirical support for its existence and importance is by now unquestionable. Nevertheless, it rarely occupies a central place in the education and training of consultants.

There are several significant implications for consultants who want to expand their knowledge, skills, and abilities by incorporating psychodynamic considerations and interventions in their work. First, unless the individual has already been exposed to these concepts and the major methods during their training or in continuing education programs, it is likely that there will be a reasonable requirement for sustained study and probably some expert coaching by a colleague who is well versed in this practice domain before the consultant would be reasonably competent. As with the application of almost any theoretical model or consulting method, significant errors in assessment, diagnosis, intervention design, or actual engagement can readily occur. Such mistakes not only can put the individual consultant at risk for reputational damage and loss of revenue when a client finds their work unsatisfactory; potentially, they also can injure the enterprise itself in a wide variety of ways.

Second, in making the decision to raise clients' awareness of these types of patterns and the importance of engaging with them, a consultant should be reasonably certain that the organization's leadership will have the necessary commitment and courage to confront the issues and work to improve them. Opening structural, process, and content challenges that were previously undiagnosed and for which there is little active motivation to address what has been identified can actually leave any institution in a worse position than if the status quo in such areas were left in place. As this chapter has pointed out repeatedly, in the majority of cases in which psychodynamic material is uncovered, the individuals, teams, and organizations making such discoveries will experience moderate to very strong emotional reactions. The containment of these emotions and directing them to the development of new and more productive patterns of behavior can take significant time and energy. Leaders are often not very motivated to undertake such sustained efforts.

Finally, even in the organizations that do the work and actually achieve significant positive changes in their relationships, operations, and performance, environmental events can readily conspire to make such gains seem irrelevant. The rise of market competitors with better technology or financing, natural disasters that destroy organizational resources, the loss of key leaders or sophisticated and expert staff, or governmental interventions can all create existentially threatening conditions and even lead to complete failure. Kilburg et al.'s (1998) model of organizational regression makes this very clear because the successful adaptation to external environments is the essential job of every leader and their team. Thus, even the best trained consultants with psychodynamic expertise must display superior and sensitive judgment before actively deploying these concepts and methods in any engagement.

6

Learning-Based Change

If the rate of change on the outside exceeds the rate of change on the inside, the end is near.

—Jack Welch (n.d.), former CEO of General Electric (Allison, 2014, p. 1)

This popular quote makes the point that change has a systems component. That is, the internal rate of change in any component of a system cannot be evaluated in isolation from the environment in which it resides or other components in that system. Put another way, even if an organization is changing, it may not be changing quickly enough if other organizations in its environment are changing more rapidly.

Furthermore, many have noted that the rate of change within the environment that most organizations reside in is increasing. A quarter century ago, Vaill (1996), using a river metaphor, noted that organizations faced continuous "whitewater" rather than a relatively smooth river flow

https://doi.org/10.1037/0000328-006
Essential Strategies for Organizational and Systems Change: An Overview for Consultants, by H. S. Leonard, R. R. Kilburg, and A. M. Freedman

with periodic moments of turbulence, and the rate of change has only accelerated since Vaill made this observation. As a consequence, companies have placed a lower priority on long-term planning and static organizational charts. Constant turbulence in organizational environments has rendered these standard planning and operational tools of limited value in an increasingly violent and unpredictable environment.

As the pace of change and the resulting turbulence increases, so too does the danger that an organization will have no other choice than to react to changes in its environment rather than anticipate them. As noted in Chapter 1, there is an active debate about whether organizations and systems have the capacity to plan and execute effective change (Demers, 2007). The optimistic belief following World War II that top-down planning could keep the organization "in front of the curve" (Bennis et al., 1969; Golembiewski, 1972) was strongly tamped down by the turmoil and crises of the following decades. Increasingly, it became clear to organizational leadership that change would not slow down, a return to "normal" was not likely, and traditional corporate planning processes were hopelessly overmatched by the accelerating changes they faced.

Furthermore, serious doubts emerged that organizations can accurately anticipate events in their environment that will require them to change and adjust to survive or take advantage of opportunities. How often are organizations, nations, and societies caught "flat-footed" in their ability to respond to events even when they are given considerable advance notice? The world is reeling from a pandemic that was accurately and widely predicted years and even decades earlier (Gates, 2015).

In recent years, organizational learning has often been viewed as a change multiplier. If organizations don't have sufficient capacity to respond effectively to current threats using known solutions and can't anticipate *and* respond to future threats, then learning-based change strategies may be the only way to keep up with, much less stay ahead of, the curve. In effect, organizations need to learn their way to success and survival because just reacting using well-known and accepted strategies is too slow and often misdirected. The rest of this chapter explores a variety of theories and strategies to facilitate as well as embed learning in the organization.

ORGANIZATIONAL LEARNING

Reginald "Reg" Revans (1983), the father of an organizational problem-solving process he termed Action Learning (AL), linked learning and change (and anticipated Welch) when he noted the central role that learning plays in organizations, stating that "learning inside must be equal to or greater than change occurring outside the organization or the organization dies" (p. 11).

Levels of Learning

Many theorists (Argot & Miron-Spektor, 2011; Marquardt, 2011; Senge, 1990; Watkins & Marsick, 1992b) have used the traditional breakdown of individual, group/team, and organization in discussing learning within organizations. *Individual learning* refers to changes within individual organizational members in skills, insights, knowledge, attitudes, and values resulting from internal and external learning opportunities through observation or experience (Crossan et al., 1999; Fiol & Lyles, 1985; Marquardt, 2011). *Team learning* involves improvement in knowledge, skills, and competencies within teams or of teams as-a-whole (Marquardt, 2011). *Organizational learning* refers to increased knowledge across the organization as a function of experience (Fiol & Lyles, 1985). Marquardt (2011) extended this definition by including "enhanced intellectual and productive capability gained through commitment to the opportunities for continuous improvement across the organization" (p. 23).

In this text, we are primarily interested in individual and group/team learning in terms of how these processes impact the success or destiny of the corporate enterprise. This focus on organizational outcomes simplifies our treatment of change, as the literature on how to develop individual and group/team learning is too large to cover in this book.

Types of Learning

We will cover in some detail, however, the various types of learning as they are directly related to organizational outcomes. Because each type of learning functions in the same way at each level of learning, we will describe each as a general type of learning without distinction to the level of learning.

Single, Double, and Deutero Learning

Argyris and Schön's (1974, 1978) well-known concepts of single- and double-loop learning are related to Bateson's (1972) notion of first- and second-order learning. *Single-loop learning* occurs when there is a recognition and correction of any deviation from an organization's underlying procedures, norms, policies, and objectives. A useful analogy is a thermostat used to control the temperature in a room or building. If the thermostat is set for 72 degrees Fahrenheit with a sensitivity of 1 degree, the heating/cooling system will be turned on or off whenever the interior temperature drops to 71 degrees or rises to 73 degrees. In other words, single-loop learning looks for and corrects according to the system's current operating principles.

Single-loop learning works well during periods of system homeostasis or steady state. Single-loop learning, however, is inadequate and, in fact, can be disastrous when "the rules of the game" quickly change without, or even with, an awareness by the organization. It has been noted that military defeats are often the result of "generals fighting the last war." In other words, military leaders accept the analysis of victory and defeat in wars immediately preceding the current war. It has also been observed that there is a danger of organizations overlearning the lessons gleaned from past crises, thus creating resistance to change and a lack of openness to new ideas or new ways to frame previous experience. From this perspective, overreliance upon "best practices" is an example of single-loop learning, perhaps to the long-term detriment of the organization.

Single-loop learning is generally the first response to disruptions to the status quo. If the organization recognizes that the old ways of doing or seeing things aren't successful, it then becomes willing to examine and change the "way we normally do things around here," resulting in *double-loop learning*. With the recognition that a more fundamental change in operations is necessary, the organization is willing to think more deeply about its assumptions and beliefs underpinning organizational behavior. In addition to examining governing principles, policies, assumptions, and beliefs, the organization may also ask questions such as these:

"Why do we exist?"
"What are our values?"
"Who are our customers?"
"Are these the customers we want?"

These questions can be profoundly philosophical as well as practical in the real world and deeply personal as well as collectively felt.

One of the inevitable consequences of double-loop learning is a change in the way individuals in the organization view themselves and their role in the organization. In this process, they often gain an appreciation of skills, knowledge, and value that they bring to the organization. Freedman (personal communication, August 20, 2021) termed this type of learning *triple-loop learning.*

Implementing single-loop learning is a fairly simple, straightforward process. The organization constantly scans for errors in the system and makes corrections when these deviations are found. Individuals only need to be trained to run the system as designed. This is usually a linear process where the transformative process (the learning) is primarily within the person being trained to run and be part of the governing system. The learner practices what is taught and receives feedback from the trainer who is the expert on how the system works.

Single-loop learning usually results in first-order change (Watzlawick et al., 1974). If the solutions that are tried always come from the same set of options, the results will always be the same, as predicted in the expression "If you do what you always did, you'll get what you always got." You will get a familiar solution that may or may not be effective depending on whether the assumptions you make about a problem are accurate.

In double-loop learning, questioning of the governing principles forces managers and trainers to develop a new "curriculum" to use when teaching organizational members how to work in the organization. We often see this shift in training and communication focus when new

CEOs take the helm of organizations promising to bring about cultural change: how we see our mission, how we treat customers, how we view safety, and so on.

Changing the governing principles of an organization, however, is much simpler in concept than in actual practice. There are many sources of resistance to change. There are threats to personal status and fears that radical changes will result in lost pay, more work, less security, and other negative outcomes. Another obstacle to fundamental change is that people are not very good at changing. This arthritic resistance to change is rooted in normal group and team process. Team members are overly deferential to status and authority (Milgram, 1974), are wedded to behaviors that worked in the past, and have vivid and painful memories of consequences of past efforts to "shake things up" (Senge, 1990). Almost everyone has reasons for being suspicious of radical changes to the governing processes of an organization.

Whereas single-loop learning is usually based on common sense and past experience, double-loop learning is most appropriate when the organization faces new and unprecedented problems where no acceptable solution is available. These situations call for second-order change (Watzlawick et al., 1974). Second-order change involves inventing new mental models and often a jump to a higher, often unique level of conceptualization. This is what T. Kuhn (1962/1996) referred to as a "paradigm shift" or "thinking outside of the box" (Loyd, 1914/2007). Double-loop learning inevitably requires creativity and new solutions.

Bateson (1972, 1979) proposed another model for learning, termed *deutero learning*, that was not a linear, one-way process with the teacher conveying truth or knowledge to the learner. He proposed an iterative process whereby the teacher facilitates and inspires learning by the student who, in turn, facilitates learning in the teacher that results in a change in their understanding of the subject being considered, and so on. Bateson described this openness to learning from the interactive process between teacher and student as being fundamental to the process of learning how to learn. This interactive process has also become central to many experiential learning processes such as AL (Leonard, 2015).

Action and Reflection

Single-loop learning doesn't normally involve reflection. The "settings" for the system are based on assumptions about the conditions in which the system runs best, given the way the system is set up. Using the thermostat analogy, occupants of the house may decide that 72 degrees is too warm and may adjust the "set" point down to 70 degrees. The system functions in the same manner, with only the inflection "set" point being changed.

The process of double-loop learning does involve reflection during the period when the governing principles are being questioned, tinkered with, and revised. Once the "new normal" has been established, however, the degree of reflection usually decreases when single-loop learning becomes dominant again.

Bateson's (1972, 1979) concept of deutero learning, however, implies that effective and continually adaptive learning requires a constant iterative process of questioning and reflecting between the teacher and learning. In fact, Bateson's notions imply that the teacher and student roles involve both teaching and learning.

Marsick and Watkins (2001) offered some useful distinctions when considering learning, action, and reflection. These authors noted that formal learning often takes place without action but usually involves some reflection on the part of the learner. Informal learning, on the other hand, usually involves action as well as reflection. Incidental learning is learning that happens in the process of just living, when there isn't an opportunity to reflect. Incidental learning, or action without reflection, is responsible for behavior without reasoning or a rational, cortical basis. Much routine behavior becomes consolidated into habits, behaviors that we don't normally think about, especially if these behaviors are consistently rewarded or punished. Over time, incidental learning can impact and modify behavior, even consolidated behaviors such as habits, if the reinforcement/punishment contingencies change.

The critical importance of reflection following action was noted by Socrates (Plato, ca. 399 BCE/2013) when he remarked, "The unexamined life is not worth living." The routine inclusion of "after-action reviews" following operations or programs is a useful way to introduce informal learning into the fabric of organizational life. The normal questioning (by students as well as teachers) that is involved in reflection following action is necessary for both double-loop and deutero learning. The inclusion of action in the learning process also sets the stage for the emergence of reflection as an important component of organizational learning.

THE LEARNING ORGANIZATION

Senge's Five Disciplines of the Learning Organization

Peter Senge (1990) is generally credited with popularizing, if not introducing, the concept of the learning organization. Senge identified four foundational disciplines present in effective learning organizations.

Personal Mastery

To attain personal mastery, one must commit themselves to a mindset of lifelong learning. This learning is not just with respect to one's professional craft and expertise but also in the personal realm—in clarifying and deepening personal vision, focusing one's energies, and developing patience, as well as having a realistic view of events. Senge referred to this mindset as the learning organization's spiritual foundation.

Mental Models

Senge (1990) referred to mental models as "deeply ingrained assumptions, generalizations, or even pictures and images that influence how we understand the world and how we take action" (p. 8). Everyone has their personal collection of mental models. Some are gained through formal, general, and professional learning. Mental models are simple and "shorthand" ways to understand events or to accomplish familiar tasks. Psychologists love their "2 × 2" figures comparing the joint effect of two variables at two levels (usually high vs. low). Teachers develop rubrics to assist in grading student performance. Lewin's (1943) force-field analysis, presented in Chapter 3, is another example of a useful mental model.

Although mental models can be useful in explaining, understanding, and simplifying our lives, they can also become outdated stereotypes without continuous examination and updating based upon the latest information. This reflection must have an internal as well as external focus. How employees see their organization is as important as how they see competitors or their business environment. This examination must be rigorous as well as courageous, balancing inquiry with advocacy while exposing and acknowledging faults, ignorance, and vulnerability.

Building Shared Vision

Virtually every great organization has been successful in developing a vision shared by employees and, in many cases, consumers about what the organization stands for and wants to accomplish. Google's vision and mission (Google, n.d.) is "to organize the world's information and make it universally accessible and useful." Ford Motor Company's vision (Ford Media, 2019) is "to become the world's most trusted company, designing smart vehicles for a smart world." Senge distinguished between a genuinely shared vision with the familiar "vision statement" generated by a task force of senior leaders. For Senge (1990), the discipline of developing a shared vision involves uncovering the "pictures of the future" (p. 9) that instill genuine commitment as opposed to enforced compliance.

Team Learning

It is interesting that this is the only foundational discipline that directly references learning. Senge (1990) observed that teams of very intelligent individuals often act as if they are a collection of dumb people. He noted the lack of effective dialogue, the inability to recognize patterns, and the instances of defensiveness and self-protectiveness.

Despite these inadequacies, Senge (1990) suggested that teams are the fundamental building blocks of organizations. To succeed and even survive, organizations need to develop methods (he used the term *technologies*) to foster team cultures that demonstrate continuous and rapid team learning. He further suggested that developing an organizational culture that values and rewards inquiry and lifelong learning is a prerequisite for team learning.

The Fifth Discipline: Systems Thinking

Whereas the previously described disciplines—personal mastery, mental models, building shared vision, and team learning—are described as discrete and foundational, the fifth discipline, systems thinking, is characterized as overarching and preeminent. Senge (1990) viewed systems thinking as the discipline that integrates the other four disciples as a sine qua non attribute of a true learning organization. Systems thinking is necessary to create a "shift of mind" in which organizational actors cease viewing themselves separately from the organization as a whole and seeing problems as having been caused by someone else. They understand how their actions create the problems that affect everyone in the organizational system. Engaging in systems thinking allows people to invent ways to create their own reality (Senge, 1990).

Argyris and Schön's Organizational Learning

Although Argyris and Schön (1974, 1978) did not offer a comprehensive model for a learning organization, they did propose several compelling theories about the factors that inhibit or promote organizational learning. These authors focused primarily on individual learning but infer and provide examples that demonstrate that the same dynamics and theories apply to social entities such as private and civic organizations and religious organizations. In the view of Argyris and Schön, individuals exhibit agency, creating cognitive models and designing action to achieve goals based on governing assumptions and values. Individuals also reflect on the consequences of their action to evaluate whether they have accomplished what they intended. In essence, according to Argyris and Schön, people are "wired" to learn. These authors also believe that organizations can act and create internal cultures that either facilitate or inhibit this inborn, natural ability to learn.

Key concepts for Argyris and Schön (1974) were "espoused theories" that include mental constructs, models, goals, and values that individuals believe they are acting in accordance with and "theories in use," what others would infer are the individual's mental constructs, models, goals, and values that produced the action they are observing and experiencing. When inconsistency is evident between what is intended (i.e., espoused theories) and how that action is interpreted by others (i.e., theories-in-use), individuals use a variety of methods to reduce the resulting cognitive tension or dissonance (Festinger, 1957). They can react defensively, for instance, by distorting or suppressing information about the consequences of actions they are displaying; or they can respond more effectively and creatively by modifying or revising how they enact their espoused theories.

Making individuals and organizations aware of the disconnects between what they intend (i.e., espoused values, goals, intentions) and what is happening and experienced by others (i.e., theories-in-use) is a key intervention, especially if moving from single-loop to double-loop learning as the most adaptive response. Without awareness and reflection, Argyris (1985) reported that most individuals display a defensive response to dissonance, termed Model I, in which the apparent values are to (a) achieve the purpose as the actor defines it; (b) win, not lose; (c) suppress negative feeling; and (d) emphasize rationality. The usual consequences of applying Model I are (a) defensive relationships, (b) low freedom of choice, (c) reduced production of valid information, and (d) little public testing of ideas (p. 89). The underlying strategy of Model I is to establish control over others to protect oneself or others by distorting or repressing reality. As one might expect, Argyris and Schön (1974) reported that organizations, reflecting the collective and cultural beliefs of their managers and employees, generally operate according to Model I.

Model I effectively restricts individuals and organizations to single-loop learning (Argyris, 1985). To reduce the defensive and limiting consequences of behaving consistently with Model I, individuals, organizations, and society need to operate according to the governing values of Model II: (a) valid information, (b) free and informed choice, and (c) internal commitment. These values are reflected in (a) shared control and (b) participation in design and implementation of action. The consequences of actually operating in Model II are (a) minimally defensive relationships, (b) high freedom of choice, and (c) increased likelihood of double-loop learning.

These authors noted, ironically, that many people, managers, and leaders who espouse Model II actually operate according to Model I. Argyris and Schön's (1974) primary intervention to facilitate movement from single to double-loop (and deutero) learning is to confront people with the discrepancies and inconsistencies between their espoused theories, intentions, and action plans and the impact of these actions on individuals in the system and the greater environment. Confrontation of these gaps combined with facilitation of a reflecting process promotes organic and natural learning that allows for a shift from normal and defensive single-loop learning to more creative and adaptive double-loop and deutero learning.

Schein's Culture and Organizational Learning

Culture is for Schein (1996b) what systems thinking is for Senge—the glue that makes organizational learning possible. Without alignment of the organizational culture with changes in the internal and external environment, anxiety and resistance will result. It is the process of working through this anxiety and resistance that allows for the development of new cultural assumptions. Learning occurs in the shift and development of cultural assumptions (Schein, 1996a).

Watkins and Marsick's Elements of Learning Organizations

Watkins and Marsick (1992a, 1992b) contributed to the theory of organizational learning by identifying fundamental elements of learning organizations: (a) continuous learning, (b) inquiry and dialogue, (c) team learning, (d) empowerment, (e) embedded systems, (f) systems connectiveness, and (g) strategic leadership. These authors, however, focused primarily on the types and levels of learning and do not discuss in any detail how to develop the processes they identify as being fundamental to learning organizations.

Marquardt—Subsystems of Learning Organizations

Best known for his model of AL, Marquardt (Marquardt et al., 2018; Marquardt et al., 2009) provided detail about how to develop learning organizations that isn't included in the earlier work of Watkins and Marsick (1992a, 1992b). Marquardt (2011) integrated the models put forth by Senge (1990), Schein (1996a, 1996b), and Watkins and Marsick (1992a, 1992b) by identifying four subsystems (organization, knowledge, people, and technology) and one overarching subsystem—learning. Five skills are identified as being fundamental to learning organizations: (a) systems thinking, (b) mental models, (c) personal mastery, (d) self-directed learning, and (e) dialogue.

PEDAGOGICAL APPROACHES TO LEARNING

Much of the previous discussion in this chapter has been about the "what" of learning—the levels, types, and descriptions of what learning organizations looks like and how they function. Senge (1990) identified factors that inhibit learning in organizations. With the exception of Bateson's deutero learning, however, the theories discussed so far give little attention to "how" people learn. Much of the analysis of learning by Argyris and Schön (1978) focused on factors that limit and those that promote effective learning. These authors, however, did not discuss in great depth how people learn or pedagogical approaches to promote learning. Many of the interventions to improve learning are based on highlighting the inconsistencies between what organizational actors are intending or striving for (espoused theories) and what they are actually doing (theories-in-use; Argyris & Schön, 1974, 1978).

Deductive/Prescriptive Versus Inductive Learning

Traditional learning is based on deductive/prescriptive learning. In this form of learning, students are given the general rules or principles for a phenomenon and are then asked to apply these rules or principles to specific situations (Gagné, 1985). Deductive learning is prescriptive, giving a model or plan for solving problems. Mental models or rubrics are often developed to help students remember and apply principles and methods to real problems. Students are often given practice exercises to reinforce theoretical models and make them concrete.

In inductive learning approaches, on the other hand, students are generally asked to take action to solve a problem or to experience a phenomenon and periodically are asked questions to help them distinguish patterns or principles (Gagné, 1985)—what did they observe, what worked, what didn't work, what they have learned, and what would they do differently the next time they are faced with similar problems or phenomena. In this manner, students create their own understandings or models that they can apply in the future. Instead of giving students mental models to apply, learners invent their own mental models.

In education, this form of learning is often described as discovery or project-based learning (Bell, 2010). Another classic example of inductive learning is what has been termed the Socratic method (Frede, 1992). Frequently used as a pedagogical device in law schools, instructors pose questions to students to stimulate critical thinking and as a way of uncovering underlying assumptions and presuppositions. The Socratic method is also used as a method for identifying better hypotheses by eliminating those that lead to contradictions.

Another benefit cited by proponents of project-based learning and the Socratic method is that these approaches are very effective in developing reasoning skills because the answer isn't immediately offered. Students are required to learn their way to knowledge by solving problems or responding to challenges offered by the teacher. In any case, the internet rendered information gathering and memorization as pointless and a waste of instructional time—gaining and storing information via the internet has become extremely easy and cheap.

Historically, most learning activities within organizations would be described as deductive/prescriptive. Because it is normal for organizations to operate in a single-loop learning environment, organizations have focused on training people to operate effectively under the prescribed vision, mission, goals, and objectives. The assumptions embedded in organizational activities and managerial directives are rarely challenged, and deviations from policies, procedures, and directives are usually punished and sanctioned. Organizations engage in double-loop learning only when they are pushed out of their "comfort zone" by disruptive events or when leadership perceives opportunities for success and growth that would require radical changes to the "way we do things around here."

Argyris and Schön's learning approach is clearly not prescriptive. By confronting discrepancies between what people intend and what they do and by encouraging reflection, inductive learning is encouraged. Argyris and Schön's (1974, 1978) intervention strategies assume that humans are naturally "wired" to learn. Given our current knowledge about human evolution, this would seem to be a well-supported assumption. For these authors, learning is a natural or normal consequence of living, solving problems, and adapting to the environmental factors facing people. In their view, although learning is natural and organic, organizations and culture can inhibit or facilitate the normal process of learning.

These authors also seemed to assume that people will behave rationally to reduce the tension or dissonance created when they are made aware of discrepancies between what they say they want or intend to do (espoused theories) and the theories that their action imply (theories-in-use; see Argyris's ladder of inference, 1990). Highlighting these discrepancies promotes reflection that, in turn, promotes personal and organizational learning.

Other authors, however, have pushed the boundaries into inductive learning further. While Argyris and Schön (1974, 1978) encouraged reflection and resolution of contradictions, they did not provide a coherent coaching or facilitation strategy to help people be better learners and more effective members of organization. An important breakthrough occurred with the integration of inductive learning processes and mental models developed to improve problem solving and human functioning that were developed by social psychologists (Kolb, 1984; Leonard, 2013), facilitation (Schwarz, 2002), adult learning (Marquardt, 2011), and team coaching (Leonard, 2015; Marquardt et al., 2009).

Experiential Learning

As noted earlier, traditionally, education and training in most fields used a deductive/prescriptive pedagogical approach. The curriculum was based on current knowledge and thinking, with the teacher/instructor providing the mental models, facts, and rubrics for students to learn. Because the content of lessons was fairly static, students were expected to commit the mental models and mathematical equations and procedures, historical facts, policies and procedures, and so on to memory. Repetitive practice exercises were generally provided to help students memorize, and periodic tests and exams were given to assess how successful the memorization had been. More advanced education (generally at the high school, college, and postgraduate level) included evaluation of students' ability to use critical thinking to apply the models, facts, mathematical procedures, policies, and procedures. This was still a deductive process. Students were tested in their ability to use current thinking and knowledge to solve problems or make predictions.

National Training Laboratories

As discussed in more detail in Chapter 3, Kurt Lewin and his students had a large influence on the development of experiential approaches to learning. Instead of sitting in classrooms with chairs lined up in rows listening to lectures given by professors, experts, and thought leaders, students might sit on the floor in a circle discussing what was going on right then, how it affected group members, and what that might mean in a theoretical yet practical sense. Termed *laboratory education*, National Training Laboratories (NTL), over several decades, developed as an experiential approach to personal, organizational, and societal change (Bradford et al., 1964).

Although formats such as the T-group strongly encouraged inductive learning, the process still included periodic "lecturettes" based on contemporary social science theory. Also, although T-groups proved to be powerful vehicles for personal learning for participants, the group process didn't directly address specific social issues or organizational problems. Some early proponents of T-groups, recognizing the gap in focusing on specific concrete problems, suggested another form of experiential group learning, termed an A-group (for application). Although this theoretical group process doesn't seem to have seen any significant implementation, the movement launched independently by Revans (1983) can be seen as a way to use experiential learning to solve complex and real problems.

While experiential learning had a great impact on the development of social psychology, especially group dynamics, team and organizational development, as well as adult learning and development, it had considerably less impact in the general field of education (Kelly, 1997). For example, Coleman (1977), although generally supporting the value and need for an experiential component in education, acknowledges the efficiency value of traditional, deductive/prescriptive, information assimilation models of learning. Coleman noted, however, that although efficient, the inductive/prescriptive and information assimilation model fails to develop much intrinsic motivation for learning. Furthermore, he noted that experiential learning is retained better because the learning is associated with concrete experience.

Kolb's Experiential Learning Theory

Kolb, a social psychologist and Lewinian, had a long association with NTL and the laboratory education movement (he attended his first T-group in 1966). Because his focus was on the individual learning process, however, his work bridges nicely with the educational community and makes the principles of experiential learning developed by the social psychological/NTL community more relevant and accessible. Kolb's well-known learning cycle (see Figure 6.1) mirrors an earlier model offered by Lewin (Kolb, 1984, p. 21).

While suggesting that the learning process normally starts with concrete experience, Kolb (1984) noted that learning can start with any of the four stages. In the prototypical experiential learning situation, the learner, either by design or circumstance, becomes immersed in a task. If this experience diverges from what they expect or is required, the learner uses reflective observation to discern what is happening. Bateson (1979) described this as a search for information, defined as looking for "differences that make a difference" (p. 76). In the third step in the inductive learning process, the learner attempts to make some sense of this information by conceptualizing and creating mental

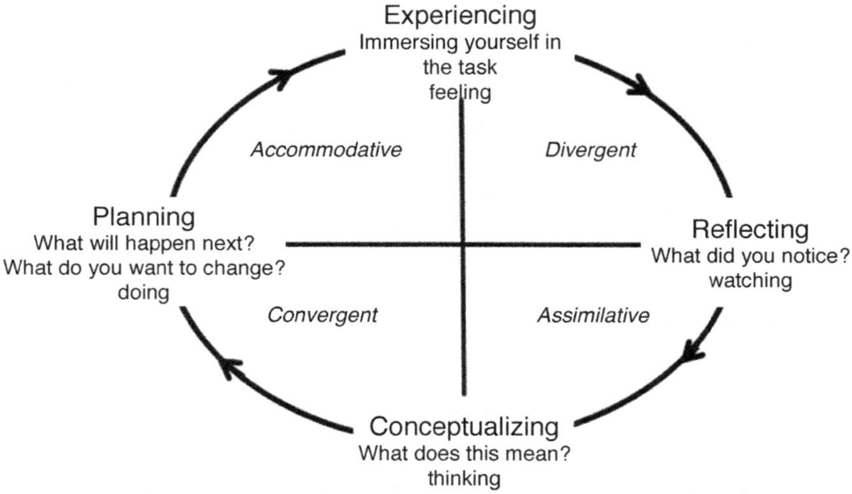

Figure 6.1

Note. Kolb's cycle of learning. From *Experiential Learning: Experience as the Source of Learning and Development* (p. 42), by D. Kolb, 1984, Prentice Hall. Copyright 1984 by Prentice Hall. Reprinted with permission.

models to explain and predict the phenomenon or experience. Using these mental models and theoretical concepts, the learner applies this learning to plan for or predict the future. This process feeds back into the learning cycle when the learner experiences the consequences of the actions taken based on the plans and predictions developed by the previous round of inductive learning. An iterative process ensues, with a reflection on the discrepancies between expected versus actual outcomes leading to a revision of the previous mental models or the creation of new theories and concepts.

One key strength of Kolb's (1984) model is that it is explicitly based on the work of some of the most prominent researchers and theorists in the 19th and 20th centuries in the fields of human learning and development: Kurt Lewin (Lewin & Gold, 1999), John Dewey (1938/1997), William James (1890/1950), Jean Piaget (see Flavell, 1963/2020), Carl Jung (1921/1971), Paulo Freire (1973), and Carl Rogers (1965a).

Kolb, synthesizing theory and research from these and other sources, distilled the following six propositions concerning learning:

1. **Learning is best conceived as a process, not in terms of outcomes.** To improve learning in higher education, the primary focus should be on engaging students in a process that best enhances their learning—a process that includes feedback on the effectiveness of their learning efforts: "education must be conceived as a continuing reconstruction of experience: . . . the process and goal of education are one and the same thing" (Dewey, 1938/1997, p. 79, as quoted in Kolb & Kolb, 2005, p. 2).
2. **All learning is relearning.** Learning is best facilitated by a process that draws out the students' beliefs and ideas about a topic so that they can be examined, tested, and integrated with new, more refined ideas (Kolb & Kolb, 2005, p. 2).
3. **Learning requires the resolution of conflicts between dialectically opposed modes of adaptation to the world.** Conflict, differences, and disagreement are what drive the learning process. In the process of learning, one is called on to move back and forth between opposing modes of reflection and action and feeling and thinking (Kolb & Kolb, 2005, p. 2).
4. **Learning is a holistic process of adaptation to the world.** It is not just the result of cognition but involves the integrated functioning of the total person—thinking, feeling, perceiving, and behaving (Kolb & Kolb, 2005, p. 2).
5. **Learning results from synergetic transactions between the person and the environment.** In Piaget's terms (Flavell, 1963/2020), learning occurs through equilibration of the dialectic processes of assimilating new experiences into existing concepts and accommodating existing concepts to new experience (Kolb & Kolb, 2005, p. 2).
6. **Learning is the process of creating knowledge.** Experiential learning theory proposes a constructivist theory of learning whereby social knowledge is created and recreated in the personal knowledge of the learner. This stands in contrast to the "transmission" model on which much current educational practice is based, where preexisting, fixed ideas are transmitted to the learner (Kolb & Kolb, 2005, p. 2).

Kolb's (1984) comprehensive and thorough integration of research and theory related to individual learning and change provides the final necessary building blocks to develop learning organizations and to create learning-based strategies for organization and systems change. Bateson (1972, 1979) and Argyris and Schön (1974) provided the technical description of types or orders of change. Senge (1990), building on decades-long development of systems theory (see Chapter 2), provided the scaffolding for promoting systems thinking. Schein (1996a, 1996b), Watkins and Marsick (1992a, 1992b), and Marquardt et al. (2018) provided the process and structure of learning organizations. Pulling all these building blocks together, Lewin (Lewin & Gold, 1999) and the NTL education movement of the 1950s and 1960s (Bradford et al., 1964) provided theory and method for promoting personal, organizational, and systems change.

Kolb's (1984) integration of the theory and practice of experiential learning laid the necessary groundwork for propelling learning-based change into the forefront of organizational and systems change (O/SC) strategies such as AL and organizational simulations (Byrnes, 2005; Corporate Executive Board, 2009). Marquardt et al. (2018), an important innovator in recent years and earlier in the area of learning organizations (Marquardt, 2011), noted that it wasn't until AL matured as an O/SC strategy that the development of true learning organizations became possible (M. J. Marquardt, personal communication, May 2, 2020).

Action Learning

As Plato (ca. 375 BCE/2013) is reputed to have noted several millennia earlier, "necessity is the mother of invention." By the end of World War II, Great Britain was in financial crisis and depleted of manpower and leadership. At the end of the war, Britain's national debt was 2.5 times its gross domestic product (GDP).[1] It had lost nearly a million men and women. Over the 30 years from World War I through World War II, Britain lost a good part of two generations of its finest leaders. Financially strapped and with greatly diminished labor and expertise, Great Britain did what it

[1] By comparison, the national debt of the United States at the end of World War II and in 2020, after taking on $2.7 trillion in debt in response to the COVID-19 pandemic, was equal to its GDP.

had to do—ask men and women to sacrifice more attractive employment to rebuild British infrastructure and financial strength. Everyone had to chip in.

Reg Revans, trained in physics and astrophysics at Cambridge and the University of Michigan, was appointed as the director of education for the National Coal Board in England immediately after World War II. Because his country was unable to pay staff in his office in the normal way—hiring expensive experts and specialized consulting firms—he instead spent several years living and working with coal miners to get a firsthand understanding of the real problems of miners and the mining industry. Out of this experience, he developed an approach that evolved into AL. Teams of nonexpert stakeholders and willing individuals were charged with working directly on critical problems through a process of inquiry and direct action. Revans referred to his colleagues in these projects as "comrades in adversity" (Revans, 1984). This was an inductive process in which action planning was based on an assessment of the impact of previous plans and actions—what was working, what needed to be improved, and how to change plans and actions going forward. Revans called this new action-focused and question-based method "Action Learning."

Several other earlier experiences shaped Revans's reservations about relying solely on prestige and authority to solve problems. As a child, Revans's father was involved in the inquiry after the sinking of the "unsinkable" HMS *Titanic* in 1912. In these investigations, it became clear that a number of the ship's architects and designers were aware of the vulnerabilities of the ship if multiple compartments were ruptured. They did not speak up because of fear of contradicting superior "experts" and appearing dumb, stupid, or unsupportive of experts or superiors.

While a member of the Cavendish Laboratories, an organization with several Nobel Prize winners, Revans (1991) observed the norm of displaying humility set by Lord Rutherford when he required participants in weekly updating discussions to reveal what wasn't going well in their labs as well as what they didn't know or understand before being allowed into discussions with other authorities and thought leaders or experts. Revans also recalled a comment by Einstein during a lecture at the labs: "If you think you understand a problem, make sure you are not deceiving yourself."[2] From these experiences, Revans (1991) learned the importance of curiosity and humility when addressing complex and complicated problems.

These experiences combined with insights he gained solving large, complex, practical problems led to the development of a process characterized by (a) the primacy of asking questions to focus discussion; (b) the inclusion of nonexperts, who aren't afraid to ask "dumb" questions; (c) humility and acknowledgment of ignorance in addressing complex and thorny problems; and, above all else, (d) a belief in the importance of taking action, experimenting, challenging orthodoxy and testing assumptions, and reflecting on the consequences to develop knowledge and wisdom. Revans (1983) emphasized this last point by stating, "There can be no learning without action, and no (sober and deliberate) action without learning" (p. 74).

Revans did not dismiss the importance of traditional knowledge learned in school, seminars, books, videos, and other formal types of training. He termed this "programmed" knowledge (Revans, 1983). He believed that programmed knowledge (P) was often the logical starting point for tackling complex problems. He strongly believed, however, that the best way to develop wisdom and understanding was to ask questions (Q). These propositions became the basis for his well-known equation: Learning (L) = *fn* (P + Q). Theorists and practitioners following Revans have added reflection (R) and implementation (I) to this expression, resulting in the following equation (Marquardt, 1999, p. 34): L = *fn* (P + Q + R + I).

Revans's formal models for AL weren't well developed until the mid-1970s and early 1980s (Revans, 1982, 1983). While NTL, T-groups, and laboratory education gained great visibility, popularity, and development in the United States in the period from 1950 to 1980, Revans struggled to be recognized or appreciated even by his countrymen and colleagues in Great Britain (Margerison, 2003). His visibility and influence have greatly

[2] This quote can be compared to Kurt Lewin's statement that "If you want to truly understand something, try to change it." Attributed to Lewin by Tolman et al. (1995, p. 31).

increased in the past three decades. The rise in the popularity of AL and the visibility and influence of Revans's ideas can be attributed to the fusion of the U.S.-based experiential learning movement inspired by NTL/ laboratory education and Kolb's experiential learning cycle and the United Kingdom/European-based AL movement developed by Revans.

Many organizational consultants recognized that AL provided the bridge between the inductive learning model proposed by earlier theorists such as Bateson (1972), Argyris and Schön (1974), Senge (1990), Schein (1996a, 1996b), Watkins and Marsick (1992a), and M. J. Marquardt (personal communication, May 2, 2020) and real-world learning organizations. In many ways, AL was an operational version of the A-group envisioned by laboratory education theorists.[3] Marquardt (personal communication, May 2, 2020) went so far as to state that "Action Learning is the best (if not the only) way to build a learning organization."

Action Learning as a Platform for Organizational and Systems Change

The AL espoused by Revans was more a framework based on fundamental principles for organizational change than a structured process of organizational and systems change. In many ways, AL can be described as pure Socratic method because of the central role of asking questions and its freedom and detachment from formal theory. Formal theory certainly has an important role in AL, but only so far as it advances and improves problem solving and learning.

AL can also be described as a platform for learning rather than as a formal theory of learning. Although the AL model is the culmination and integration of many decades of theory involving inductive and experiential learning, it is not, by itself, a problem-solving model. A familiar metaphor may help the reader understand this fundamental characteristic of AL. Consider a computer operating system such as Microsoft Windows. By itself, Windows does little of practical value. Its central value is to allow users to access other, more practical applications such as word processors,

[3] This is also the model that is promoted by the World Institute of Action Learning (WIAL) and used in their training. Skipton Leonard and Arthur Freedman were among the group that founded WIAL. More information about this model can be found at https://www.wial.org.

spreadsheets, or databases that allow the user to complete certain tasks. Like Windows, AL is primarily concerned with how work is getting done and not with the work itself.

In AL, all discussions begin with questions to stimulate reflection that will create linkages among knowledge, skill sets, or experiences that have been useful to individuals in the past. The beauty of AL is that individuals don't need to discard or unlearn anything that was useful in the past, whether it was in the classroom or on the playground. Even knowledge, skills, or experiences that have not been successful for individuals can be useful in assessing and predicting what will be successful in the future. Figure 6.2 provides an illustration of AL as a platform for team problem solving and learning, wherein prior sources of knowledge can support the AL process. In this example, knowledge held by AL team members or that potentially can be accessed by team members can be applied to solving the problem accepted by the team.

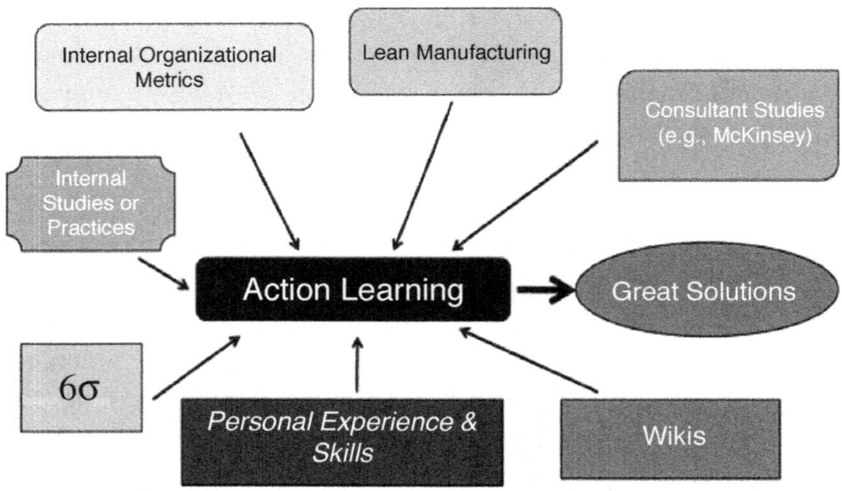

Figure 6.2

Note. Action learning as a platform for team problem solving and learning. From *Great Solutions Through Action Learning: Success Every Time* (p. 37), by H. S. Leonard and A. M. Freedman, 2013, Learning Thru Action Press. Copyright 2013 by Learning Thru Action Press. Reprinted with permission.

Flipping the World on Its Head—Rethinking Our Approach to Living and Learning

The learning models described here, and exemplified by AL, turn the traditional pedagogical approach upside down and on its head. The traditional teaching and training approach is to (a) present a concept or skill, (b) provide exercises to facilitate memorization of material or to practice the skill, and (c) test for retention of the knowledge or mastery of the skill. If the learner fails at the third step, the process is repeated until some minimal level of retention or proficiency is attained. Most experiential training models used in education and business follow this model when they use brief content presentations ("lecturettes") followed by "experiential" exercises to provide practice opportunities.

The pedagogical model used in AL reverses the order in the learning process. Following Kolb (1984), the learner is (a) engaged in a problem with minimal preparation or direction, (b) provided with frequent and periodic opportunities for debriefing (what is working, can be improved, and could be done differently), (c) asked to conceptualize and create mental models to make sense of their experience, and (d) asked to make a plan to solve the problem that takes into account what has been learned.

Immersive Learning—The Value of Highly Realistic Organizational Simulations

Organizational leadership simulations (OLSs) immerse participants in a highly realistic simulated organizational environment that requires them to take individual and collective action to solve a set of problems or a critical situation facing the organization. Participants in an OLS must work together effectively to achieve organizational objectives. OLS coaches promote inductive learning by leading debriefing and after-action-review processes.

As a learning strategy, OLSs and AL have complementary strengths. AL is very effective in developing the leadership competencies required to solve the particular problem(s) facing the organization (Leonard & Lang, 2010). The organization, however, doesn't have control over the required competencies before the team addresses the problem(s). Simulations, on the other hand, can be designed to require specific leadership competencies based on the contextual information provided to each participant leader. Because of the complementary nature of AL and OLSs, they are easily and successfully combined in larger leadership development programs (Leonard & Goff, 2003).

Action Learning Case Study—Developing Leadership Competencies While Solving Real Problems

AL is often included in corporate executive development programs as a way of developing plans to solve corporate problems that are complex, critical, unprecedented, or unexpected and for which the organization does not have any current or acceptable solutions (Marquardt et al., 2009). These are the sort of problems described in Chapter 4 as requiring radical changes in the way the organization is used to working.

In response to the 2008 financial crisis, the U.S. government authorized the expenditure of $426.4 billion through the Troubled Asset Relief Program (TARP) to stabilize the country's financial system, restore economic growth, and mitigate foreclosures (Segal, 2020). The opportunities for graft, corruption, misappropriation of funds, and failure to repay loans in this situation were enormous, based on results from earlier government investments of this scale in response to previous crises (Encyclopedia, n.d.).

Faced with these challenges and financial dangers, the Department of Commerce (DOC) tasked three AL teams formed with participants in an ongoing executive leadership development program (senior executive service level) to develop strategies and plans to mitigate the financial, legal, and political risks related to a program of this scale (Leonard & Lang, 2010). Each team typically met once a week for 3 to 4 months. Each team was provided with a professionally trained AL coach[4] who intervened by asking probing questions whenever they recognized an opportunity

[4] Each coach was certified as an AL coach through WIAL. Many of the coaches were trained by Skipton Leonard and Arthur Freedman, both Master Action Learning Coaches for WIAL. Detailed description of the AL practices used in this program is provided by Leonard and Freedman (2013).

to improve team problem-solving performance. Each AL team had two objectives: (a) to provide a written report that outlines the recommendations of the team and (b) to make a formal presentation detailing the key recommendations in the written report. Several of the recommendations were ultimately folded into the ongoing policies and practices developed by DOC leadership.

The final TARP implementation plan created with input from the AL teams (a) stabilized the global banking system, (b) probably saved the U.S. auto industry, (c) saved a million jobs, and (d) contributed an additional $15.3 billion to the U.S. Treasury from interest on loans and appreciation of investments (Segal, 2020). In addition, although there was criticism of the choice of companies that were funded by TARP or the speed of distribution of appropriated money to needy homeowners or businesses, there were few reports of graft, corruption, or misappropriation of funds (Segal, 2020). The program also provided significant training and experience in solving complex and critical problems with "high-stakes" outcomes (Leonard & Lang, 2010).

IMPLICATIONS FOR CONSULTING PRACTICE: USING LEARNING-BASED ORGANIZATIONAL CHANGE STRATEGIES

Organizational consulting has gone through a period of profound change since the end of World War II. Before that, organizational consultants prescribed methods and actions to be taken to address problems or to achieve goals and objectives. These methods and actions were based on knowledge developed slowly over long periods of time, often centuries. When the models no longer worked or where no models were available, new theories, reluctantly, were developed by O/SC theorists and practitioners. The new models then became the accepted orthodoxy. Most organizational change was brought about by political change, military conquests, or quantum jumps in technological inventions. Between these events, nations, society, and organizations experienced long periods of homeostasis or dynamic equilibrium. During these periods, single-loop learning predominated, simplifying the process of organizational consultation. Prescriptive advice and solutions were all that was desired or needed.

The horrors of world and nuclear wars, as well as rapid technological advances in science, communication, medicine, and transportation, have promoted the integration and globalization of problems and human efforts. These processes have resulted in the "permanent whitewater" noted by Vaill (1996) a quarter of a century ago. The theories and models that have been presented in this chapter provide useful methods and road maps for consultation designed to promote double-loop and deutero learning, develop learning organizations, and foster inductive-learning approaches to organizational problem solving and organizational change.

The development of laboratory education, inspired by Kurt Lewin, was based on experiential and inductive learning. Many of the prominent thought leaders in organizational learning such as Argyris and Schön (1974, 1978), Schein (1996a), and Senge (1990) were strongly influenced by the methodologies developed at NTL in the 1950s and 1960s. Although many of the theories and mental models became the foundations for common practices in OD (see Chapters 3 and 4) and continued to be useful in programs for personal and team development such as T-groups, team-building, and organizational learning, they did not find widespread usefulness in creating learning organizations until the advent of AL and OLSs. As M. J. Marquardt (personal communication, May 2, 2020) noted, the creation of true learning organizations became possible only after widespread application of AL.

Integration of the body of knowledge and practice of the laboratory education/experiential learning movement in the United States, represented by Kolb's (1984) work, and the AL movement in the United Kingdom and Europe, represented by the work of Revans (1983), provided the impetus for Marquardt and others (Marquardt, 1999; Marquardt et al., 2009) to develop a structured and systematic approach to organizational and systems change such as AL. Other immersive and inductive learning-based approaches to organizational change and leadership development such as OLSs are also now available to organizational consultants (Leonard & Hill, 2021).

7

Positive Psychology, Behaviorism, and Neuropsychology and the Future of Organizational and Systems Change

Although positive psychology, behaviorism, and neuropsychology all have had significant impact on the application of psychology in organizations, the theories discussed in this chapter are not covered in depth because they don't include a systematic and coherent model for organizational and systems change (O/SC) and can't easily or seamlessly be included into one of the other change strategies presented in this text. The theories that are presented in this chapter do, however, provide partial models of change that may be of value and interest to consulting psychologists. They may also provide fruitful starting material for more fully developed O/SC theory in the future.

https://doi.org/10.1037/0000328-007
Essential Strategies for Organizational and Systems Change: An Overview for Consultants, by H. S. Leonard, R. R. Kilburg, and A. M. Freedman

POSITIVE PSYCHOLOGY

Maslow (1954) used the term *positive psychology* to refer to psychological theory that emphasizes growth, development, and human potential, in contrast to the prevailing Freudian theory based on a medical model that focused on disfunction, disease, and disability. Maslow was also greatly influenced by Lewin and his emphasis on assessing the current state of the psychological field rather than a backward-looking analysis of a person's physical and mental development.

Seligman (1998) suggested a new field of psychology devoted to a positive study of behavior and psychology in his American Psychological Association presidential speech in 1998. The positive psychology movement emphasizes those factors that promote happiness, well-being, quality of life, contentment, creativity, a sense of personal purpose, and a positive mindset (Deiner, 2009; Seligman, 2002; Seligman & Csikszentmihalyi, 2000). Broadly speaking, most of the principles of the positive psychology movement are consistent with the principles of organization development (OD) and change management (CM), and most organizational consultants using those change strategies would agree with and embrace the positive psychology perspective.

APPRECIATIVE INQUIRY

A good example of the synergy between positive psychology principles and O/SC is the *appreciative inquiry* (AI) movement (Cooperrider, 1999). Cooperrider's (1999) critique of OD practice in the last decades of the 20th century was that consultants placed too much emphasis on problems facing the organization or system and not enough on the vision of what was possible (see Beckhard's OD model, 1969; Figure 3.4, this volume). From this perspective, too much of OD practice is focused on what is wrong and what needs to be fixed rather than on what works, what the organization's or system's positive attributes are, and what people really care about. Cooperrider and Whitney (2001) described four key processes in AI as follows:

1. Discovering—identifying organizational processes that work well
2. Dreaming—envisioning processes that would work well in the future

3. Designing—planning and prioritizing those processes that would work well
4. Deploying—executing the proposed design (p. 5)

A central goal of AI is to build or rebuild organizations around what works rather than trying to fix what is broken. As an example of how this AI principle is used in practice, Leonard and Freedman (2013) recommended that Action Learning coaches use debriefing questions such as "What is working well?" and "How can these processes be improved even further?"

BEHAVIORAL MODELS OF CHANGE

Behavioral models for behavior change have been around since the early to mid-20th century, and many behavioral principles are so solidly embedded in organizational practices and policies that we hardly notice them.[1] For instance, the extensive use of rewards and incentives to shape desired behavior and punishment and sanctions to stop or extinguish undesirable behavior was inspired by the work of behaviorists such as Skinner (Ferster & Skinner, 1957). Likewise, classical Pavlovian principles (e.g., pairing a neutral object or event with an event that elicits a predictable response [e.g., pleasure, fear, desire] to obtain a "conditioned" response [Pavlov, 1927]) are used in a variety of ways to elicit emotional reactions, attitudes, and involuntary behavioral responses.

Behaviorism is also associated with a focus on behavioral rather than internal mental operations to understand behavior or bring about change (Watson, 1930). In contrast to psychoanalytic and Gestalt psychology, early behaviorists displayed little interest in mental thoughts, images, emotion, or attitudes as antecedents to change. They demonstrated that behavioral change or behavior modification could be affected by identifying a behavioral goal and applying behavioral change principles such as the

[1] Portions of the text for this section are from "The History and Current Status of Organizational and Systems Change," by H. S. Leonard, in H. S. Leonard, R. Lewis, A. M. Freedman, and J. Passmore (Eds.), *The Wiley-Blackwell Handbook of the Psychology of Leadership, Change, and Organizational Development* (pp. 257–258), 2013, Wiley-Blackwell UK (https://doi.org/10.1002/9781118326404.ch12). Copyright 2013 by Wiley-Blackwell UK. Reprinted with permission.

use of rewards and punishment to shape and strengthen the desired behavioral goal (Martin & Pear, 2014).

In recent years, there has been an integration of cognitive/mental and behavioral change models to bring about specific behavioral goals (Rachman, 1997). An example of this integrative approach is the *transtheoretical model* (TTM) for treating habitual or addictive behaviors, traditionally considered some of the most difficult behaviors to change (Prochaska & DiClemente, 1994). These authors have identified the following stages in the change process for these types of behaviors: precontemplation, contemplation, preparation, action, and maintenance. The TTM approach provides cognitive and behavioral learning activities to address the known obstacles to behavioral change.

While change models such as the TTM (Prochaska & Norcross, 2002) show promise, it remains to be demonstrated that these methods can be useful in large-scale systems change initiatives. Cognitive behavioral methods are best used in first-order change environments where change agents have a good understanding of the cognitive conditions and behavioral reinforcers that maintain the current undesirable behavior and that need to be changed to bring about the desired behaviors. These generally are not unpredictable and unstable environments demonstrating nonlinear systems effects that require second-order change strategies.

NEUROSCIENCE AND CHANGE

Recent advances in the understanding of neuroscience provide us with a better understanding of the person in Lewin's expression of the relationship between behavior (B), the person (P), and the environment (E) at any given time: B = *fn* (P, E).[2] With the exception of psychoanalytic approaches, most change theories assume that people make more or less rational decisions as either change agents or as the objects of change.

[2] Portions of the text for this section are from "The History and Current Status of Organizational and Systems Change," by H. S. Leonard, in H. S. Leonard, R. Lewis, A. M. Freedman, and J. Passmore (Eds.), *The Wiley-Blackwell Handbook of the Psychology of Leadership, Change, and Organizational Development* (pp. 258–260), 2013, Wiley-Blackwell UK (https://doi.org/10.1002/9781118326404.ch12). Copyright 2013 by Wiley-Blackwell UK. Reprinted with permission.

Emotional responses such as fear are assumed to be rational responses to the dangers involved in change. Furthermore, people are expected to make rational decisions based on the expectation that a certain response will result in the largest benefit in relation to the costs involved.

Economic models in the latter part of the 20th century assumed a perfectly rational marketplace that, almost mysteriously, factored in all the relevant variables in establishing prices and making economic decisions in markets (e.g., the efficient market hypothesis; Fama, 1965). Counter-arguments that economic decisions were not always made on the basis of cool-headed rational analysis (individually or collectively) were strengthened by analyses of the emotionally exaggerated decisions of investors in the run-up "bubble" of 2004 to 2006 followed by the panic selling of late 2008 (Fox, 2009).

Early theories of why people failed to maximize their self-interest in many situations as Adam Smith (1776/2003) predicted pointed to the archaic functioning of the brain's limbic system (cf. Bernstein & Rosen, 1990). The reasoning behind these explanations was that primitive emotions (e.g., fear, rage, greed, lust) controlled by neural structures in the limbic system overwhelmed the more reasonable and rational neocortex, leading to actions that may have some value in terms of short-term protection and gratification but that, in the longer term, were dysfunctional.

These arguments, however, were less persuasive when neuroscience discovered that there were much more complex relationships between various limbic structures and cortical structures, specifically the prefrontal cortex (Damasio, 1994, 1999). Damasio's research indicated that limbic structures play an intermediating role between perceptual organs and the brain in "marking" input that is of potential harm or benefit to the individual. This information is then passed through a rich neural network to the prefrontal cortex for further processing and decision making. The results of this neural processing are then sent back through the limbic structures for muscular and motoric action.

Effective behavior requires successful integration of both the limbic system and the prefrontal cortex. The prefrontal cortex has been described as responsible for "executive" functioning and is the last area of the brain to mature, often in a person's 20s. Wilson (1998) noted that "without the stimulus and guidance of emotion, rational thought slows and disintegrates" (p. 113). Pinker (1997) commented further on the connections between the archaic "dinosaur" brain of the limbic system and the more recently developed prefrontal cortical structures: "Intelligence is the pursuit of goals in the face of obstacles . . . emotions are mechanisms that set the brain's highest-level goals . . . emotion triggers the cascade of subgoals and sub-subgoals that we call thinking and acting" (pp. 372–373).

The recently acquired understanding of neural functioning has been applied to change in several ways. Rock (2009) provided a synthesis of all brain functioning (all paleo and neocortical structures) to provide insight on the impact of neural processes on behavior. The expressed purpose of these accounts is to help everyone, no matter their position or situation, understand their own reactions and behaviors as well as those of the people whom they come in contact or deal with, helping them become more successful and productive as leaders, team members, and employees. This information has broad usefulness in the discussion of change and personal coaching (Rock & Page, 2009) but is not structured sufficiently to provide specific guidance for larger scale change efforts.

Lawrence and Nohria (2002) and Lawrence (2010) have taken a more focused approach to the new brain research, examining the relationship between limbic and prefrontal cortex structures to posit a small group of primary motives that must be attended to if change agents are to capture the "hearts and minds" of those who must implement or will be the objects of the intended change. Earlier in his career, Lawrence had become well known for his analytic/rational approach to organizational differentiation and integration (Lawrence & Lorsch, 1969). His most recent research represents a more balanced treatment of analytic/rational and emotional factors involved in organizational behavior.

This research also integrates the emerging work of evolutionary psychology (Buss, 1999; Pinker, 1994) with the clinical findings of neuropsychology, some of which have already been described here (i.e., Damasio, 1999). Using a neo-Darwinian argument, Lawrence and Nohria (2002) and Lawrence (2010) argued that the process of genetic variation, selection for survival, and retention through successful breeding account for a group of four primary drives or motives that are innately determined and operationalized through the limbic–prefrontal cortex system: (a) acquisition, (b) bonding, (c) learning, and (d) defending.[3] Lawrence's work should be a reminder to anyone contemplating or planning change to take into consideration basic and innate human needs.

IMPLICATIONS FOR CONSULTING PRACTICE: USING POSITIVE PSYCHOLOGY, APPRECIATIVE INQUIRY, BEHAVIORAL THEORY, AND NEUROSCIENCE IN PRACTICE

Although none of these theories provide comprehensive road maps, elements of each are often useful in consulting practice. For instance, positive psychology has fundamentally altered how coaching is perceived and used. Before the 1990s coaching strategies were primarily recommended for individuals in danger of "derailing" or failing in their current role. In contemporary organizations, coaching is often recommended for "high-potential" leaders or for preparing managers or executives for challenging promotions. The impact of appreciative inquiry can be seen in the way the "problems" in past years have become the "challenges" of today.

In the behavior realm, organizations are constantly looking for ways to motivate employees beyond pay and promotion. The influence of Maslow (1954) and job satisfaction research (Herzberg, 2003) can easily be seen in these "enlightened" management strategies and practices.

Finally, although the difficulty in operationalizing neuroscience concepts in standard management practices has limited their influence in

[3] Earlier, Freud (1930/2005), on the basis of his clinical work, had posited that "The communal life of human beings had, therefore, a two-fold foundation: the compulsion to work, which was created by external necessity, and the power of love" (p. 48). Lawrence's list of innate drives can also be compared to Maslow's hierarchy of needs (1954), which have gained almost universal currency in explaining human motivation. Lawrence assumes that activation of these four drives in coordination with an effective prefrontal cortical response will ensure the best fit of the individual with the environment, which therefore results in successful competition of their genes with the genes of others in the propagation of the species. Both Freud's and Maslow's observations and theories can be accounted for using Lawrence's four-drive theory. Some might argue that Maslow's highest level need, self-actualization, is superordinate, and therefore separate, from the practical need to learn in the pursuit of successful adaptation to the environment. The fact that Maslow found so few individuals who were truly self-actualized provides a counter, perhaps cynical, argument for the differentiation of Maslow's need for self-actualization and Lawrence's drive to learn.

board rooms, the general acceptance of the importance of these processes in everyday life makes it likely that practical theories based on neuroscience will emerge in the future.

THE FUTURE OF ORGANIZATIONAL/SYSTEMS CHANGE THEORY AND PRACTICE

The organizational/systems change (O/SC) strategies presented in this book are based on most of the significant theoretical approaches and practices provided by contemporary psychology: systems theory; Lewinian, OD, and CM approaches; family systems; Freudian/psychodynamic; and learning-based models. This chapter has also discussed the important influences of positive psychology, behavioral models, and neuropsychology.

We predict that the future of O/SC theory and practice will include the further integration of all these approaches as research evidence demonstrates their usefulness in their study and practice of organizational consulting. Our own evolution of the thinking and practice demonstrate this breaking down of barriers between the many schools of O/SC theory and practice. Leonard, trained as a social and organizational psychologist with a strong systems and group dynamics perspective, is also a strong advocate and practitioner of Action Learning. In addition to having a strong interest and background in psychodynamic theory and practice, Kilburg is also a proponent of systems theory and OD in the proper context. Freedman began his journey as a clinical psychologist and later became a strong contributor and thought leader in the OD and Action Learning movements. We expect to see more of this integration of theory and practice as the field of O/SC evolves.

References

Ainsworth, M. D. S. (1969). Object relations, dependency, and attachment: A theoretical review of the infant–mother relationship. *Child Development, 40*(4), 969–1025. https://doi.org/10.2307/1127008

Ainsworth, M. D. S., Blehar, M., Waters, E., & Wall, S. (1978). *Patterns of attachment.* Lawrence Erlbaum Associates.

Allison, S. (2014). *The responsive organization: Coping with new technology and disruption.* https://www.forbes.com/sites/scottallison/2014/02/10/the-responsive-organization-how-to-cope-with-technology-and-disruption/?sh=63f3c0c33cdd

Allport, F. H. (1962). A structuronomic conception of behavior: Individual and collective. I. Structural theory and the master problem of social psychology. *Journal of Abnormal and Social Psychology, 64*(1), 3–30. https://doi.org/10.1037/h0043563

American Psychiatric Association. (1980). *A psychiatric glossary* (5th ed.). Little, Brown & Company.

Argot, L., & Miron-Spektor, E. (2011). Organizational learning: From experience to knowledge. *Organization Science, 22*(5), 1123–1137. https://doi.org/10.1287/orsc.1100.0621

Argyris, C. (1962). *Interpersonal competence and organizational effectiveness.* Dorsey.

Argyris, C. (1970). *Intervention theory and method.* Addison-Wesley.

Argyris, C. (1985). *Strategy, change and defensive routines.* Pitman Publishing.

Argyris, C., & Schön, D. (1974). *Theory in practice: Increasing professional effectiveness.* Jossey-Bass.

Argyris, C., & Schön, D. (1978). *Theory in practice: Increasing professional effectiveness* (reprint ed.). Jossey-Bass.

Asch, S. E. (1951). Effects of group pressure upon the modification and distortion of judgments. In H. Guetzkow (Ed.), *Groups, leadership and men; research in human relations* (pp. 177–190). Carnegie Press.

Ashby, W. (1958). General systems theory as a new discipline. *General Systems Yearbook, 3*, 1–6.

Bales, R. F. (1970). *Personality and interpersonal behavior*. Holt, Rinehart and Winston.

Bateson, G. (1972). *Steps to the ecology of mind*. Ballantine Books.

Bateson, G. (1979). *Mind and nature*. Bantam Books.

Bateson, G., Jackson, D. D., Haley, J., & Weakland, J. (1956). Toward a theory of schizophrenia. *Behavioral Science, 1*(4), 251–264. https://doi.org/10.1002/bs.3830010402

Bazerman, M. H., & Watkins, M. D. (2008). *Predictable surprises: The disasters you should have seen coming and how to prevent them*. Harvard Business Press.

Beckhard, R. (1969). *Organization development: Strategies and models*. Addison Wesley.

Beckhard, R., & Harris, R. T. (1987). *Organization transitions: Managing complex change* (2nd ed.). Addison Wesley.

Bell, S. (2010). Project-based learning for the 21st century: Skills for the future. *The Clearing House: A Journal of Educational Strategies, Issues and Ideas, 83*(2), 39–43. https://doi.org/10.1080/00098650903505415

Benjamin, J. (2011, October 20). Containing excess: Sexuality, attachment, and intersubjectivity in theory and transference. *The Scientific Meetings of the AIP*. https://doi.org/10.1057/ajp.2012.3

Bennis, W. G., Benne, K. D., & Chin, R. (Eds.). (1969). *The planning of change*. Holt, Rinehart and Winston. https://doi.org/10.1097/00000446-196908000-00051

Bennis, W. G., & Shepard, H. (1956). A theory of group development. *Human Relations, 9*(4), 415–437. https://doi.org/10.1177/001872675600900403

Benson, J. K. (1977). Organizations: A dialectic view. *Administrative Science Quarterly, 22*(1), 1–21. https://doi.org/10.2307/2391741

Bernstein, A. J., & Rosen, S. C. (1990). *Dinosaur brains*. Ballantine Books.

Bion, W. R. (1989). *Experiences in groups and other papers*. Routledge. (Original work published 1961)

Blake, R., & Mouton, J. (1964). *The managerial grid: The key to leadership excellence*. Gulf Publishing Co.

Block, P. (2011). *Flawless consulting* (3rd ed.). Pfeiffer/Wiley.

Blofeld, J. (1968). *I Ching. The book of changes*. E P Dutton.

Boring, E. G. (1950). *A history of experimental psychology* (2nd ed.). Prentice-Hall.

Boudreau, J. W., & Ramstad, P. M. (2007). *Beyond HR: The new science of human capital*. Harvard Business Review Press.

Boulding, K. (1960). Towards a general theory as a new discipline. *General Systems Yearbook, 5*, 66–75.

Bowen, M. (1976). Theory in the practice of psychotherapy. In P. J. Guerin, Jr. (Ed.), *Family therapy* (pp. 42–90). Gardner Press.

Bowlby, J. (1988). *A secure base*. Basic Books.

Bradford, L. P. (1967). Biography of an institution. *The Journal of Applied Behavioral Science, 3*(2), 127–143. https://doi.org/10.1177/002188636700300203

Bradford, L. P., Gibb, J. R., & Benne, K. D. (Eds.). (1964). *T-Group theory and laboratory method: Innovation in re-education*. John Wiley & Sons.

Brenner, C. (1976). *Psychoanalytic technique and psychic conflict*. International Universities Press.

Brenner, C. (1982). *The mind in conflict*. International University Press.

Burgess, R. G. (1984). *In the field: An introduction to field research*. George Allen & Unwin.

Burns, T., & Stalker, G. M. (1961). *The management of innovation*. Tavistock.

Buss, D. (1999). *Evolutionary psychology: The new science of the mind*. Allyn & Bacon.

Butz, M. R. (1997). *Chaos and complexity: Implications for psychological theory and practice*. Taylor & Francis.

Byrnes, N. (2005, October 10). Star search: How to recruit, train, and hold on to great people: What works, what doesn't. *Business Week*, 71.

Campbell, J. P., & Dunnette, M. D. (1968). Effectiveness of T-group experiences in managerial training and development. *Psychological Bulletin, 70*(2), 73–104. https://doi.org/10.1037/h0026031

Carr, A., & Gabriel, Y. (2001). The psychodynamics of organizational change management: An overview. *Journal of Organizational Change Management, 14*(5), 415–421. https://doi.org/10.1108/EUM0000000005872

Cartwright, D., & Zander, A. (Eds.). (1968). *Group dynamics: Research and theory* (3rd ed.). Harper & Row.

Center for Workplace Development. (2022). *Organization development consulting*. https://hr.harvard.edu/organizational-development

Channon, D. F., & Cooper, A. A. (2015). McKinsey's model. In C. L. Cooper, J. McGee, & T. Sammut-Bonnici (Eds.), *Wiley encyclopedia of management: Vol. 12. Strategic management* (pp. 1–2). John Wiley & Sons. https://doi.org/10.1002/9781118785317.weom120005

Child, J. (1997). Strategic choice in the analysis of action, structure, organizations and environment: Retrospective and prospect. *Organization Studies, 18*(1), 43–76. https://doi.org/10.1177/017084069701800104

Christian, C. (2015). Intersubjectivity and modern conflict theory. *Psychoanalytic Psychology, 32*(4), 608–625. https://doi.org/10.1037/pap0000011

Coleman, J. A. (1977). Differences between experiential and classroom learning. In M. T. Keeton (Ed.), *Experiential learning. Rationale characteristics, and assessment* (pp. 49–61). Jossey-Bass.

Cooperrider, D. (1999). *Appreciative inquiry: Rethinking human organization toward a positive theory of change*. Stipes Publishing.

Cooperrider, D. L., & Whitney, D. (2001). A positive revolution in change. In D. L. Cooperrider, P. Sorenson, D. Whitney, & T. Yeager (Eds.), *Appreciative Inquiry: An emerging direction for organization development* (pp. 9–29). Stipes.

Corporate Executive Board. (2009, March 19). What drives leadership bench strength? *Learning and Development Roundtable*. Corporate Executive Board.

Cronin, G., & Andrews, S. (2009). After action reviews: A new model for learning. *Emergency Nurse, 17*(3), 32–35. https://doi.org/10.7748/en2009.06.17.3.32.c7090

Crossan, M. M., Lane, H. W., & White, R. E. (1999). An organizational learning framework: From intuition to institution. *Academy of Management Review, 24*(3), 522–537. https://doi.org/10.5465/amr.1999.2202135

Cummings, T. G., & Worley, C. G. (2015). *Organization development and change* (10th ed.). South-Western Cengage Learning.

Czander, W. M. (1993). *The psychodynamics of work and organizations: Theory and application*. Guilford Press.

Dalton, J. H., Elias, M. J., & Wandersman, A. (2001). *Community psychology*. Wadsworth/Thomson Learning.

Damasio, A. (1994). *Descartes' error: Emotion, reason, and the human brain*. Putnam.

Damasio, A. (1999). *The feeling of what happens: Body and emotion in the making of consciousness*. Harcourt Brace.

Darwin, C. (1859). *On the origin of species by means of natural selection, or the preservation of favoured races in the struggle for life*. John Murray. https://doi.org/10.5962/bhl.title.82303

Davenport, T. (1995, October). The fad that forgot people. *Fast Company, 1*, 70–75.

Deiner, E. (2009). Positive psychology: Past, present, and future. In S. J. Lopez & C. R. Snyder (Eds.), *The Oxford handbook of positive psychology* (pp. 7–11). Oxford University Press.

Demers, C. (2007). *Organizational change theories*. Sage Publications.

Deming, W. E., & Orsini, J. (Eds.). (2012). *The essential Deming: Leadership principles from the father of quality*. McGraw-Hill.

Dewey, J. (1997). *Experience and education* (Delta Kappa Pi Lecture). Touchstone. (Original work published 1938)

Diamond, M. A. (1993). *The unconscious life of organizations: Interpreting organizational identity*. Quorum Books.

Durkheim, E. (1982). The psychological character of social facts and their reality. In S. Lukes (Ed.), *The rules of sociological method* (pp. 249–250). Palgrave. (Original work published 1895)

Dyer, W. G. (1987). *Team building: Issues and alternatives*. John Wiley & Sons.
Emanuel, R. (2009, January 28). A 40-year wish list. *The Wall Street Journal*, p. 14.
Emery, F. E., & Trist, E. L. (1960). Socio-technical systems. In *Management science models and techniques* (Vol. 2). Pergamon Press.
Emery, F. E., & Trist, E. L. (1965). The causal texture of organizational environments. *Human Relations, 18*(1), 21–32. https://doi.org/10.1177/001872676501800103
Encyclopedia. (n.d.). Profiteering. In *Encyclopedia.com*. Retrieved September 23, 2022, from https://www.encyclopedia.com/defense/energy-government-and-defense-magazines/profiteering
Fama, E. (1965). The behavior of stock market prices. *The Journal of Business, 38*(1), 34–105. https://doi.org/10.1086/294743
Fayol, H. (1949). *General and industrial management* (J. A. Coubrough, Trans.). Sir Isaac Pitman & Sons.
Fermi, E. (1956). *Thermodynamics*. Dover Publications.
Ferster, C. B., & Skinner, B. F. (1957). *Schedules of reinforcement*. Appleton-Century-Crofts. https://doi.org/10.1037/10627-000
Festinger, L. (1954). A theory of social comparison processes. *Human Relations, 7*(2), 117–140. https://doi.org/10.1177/001872675400700202
Festinger, L. (1957). *A theory of cognitive dissonance*. Stanford University Press. https://doi.org/10.1515/9781503620766
Fiol, C. M., & Lyles, M. A. (1985). Organizational learning. *Academy of Management Review, 10*(4), 803–813. https://doi.org/10.2307/258048
Flavell, J. A. (2020). *The developmental psychology of Jean Piaget*. Barakaldo Books. (Original work published 1963)
Fox, J. (2009). *Myth of the rational market*. Harper Business.
Frede, M. (1992). Plato's arguments and the dialogue form. *Oxford studies in ancient philosophy, supplementary* (Vols. 201–19). Cambridge University Press.
Freedman, A. M. (1997). The undiscussable sides of implementing transformational change. *Consulting Psychology Journal, 49*(1), 51–76. https://doi.org/10.1037/1061-4087.49.1.51
Freedman, A. M. (2006). Action research: Origins and application for OD&C practitioners. In M. Brazzel & B. B. Jones (Eds.), *The NTL handbook of organization development and change* (pp. 7–13). Jossey-Bass/NTL Institute.
Freedman, A. M. (2017). *Leading radical change in complex organizations: A field book* (in collaboration with C. Jules). ClearSpace.
Freeman, R. E. (1984). *Strategic management: A stakeholder approach*. Pitman.
Freire, P. (1973). *Education for critical consciousness*. Seabury Press.
French, J., & Raven, B. (1968). The bases of social power. In D. Cartwright & A. Zander (Eds.), *Group dynamics: Research and theory* (pp. 259–269). Harper & Row.
French, W. L., & Bell, C. (1973). *Organization development: Behavioral science interventions for organization improvement*. Prentice-Hall.

French, W. L., & Bell, C. (1984). *Organization development: Behavioral science interventions for organization improvement* (3rd ed.). Prentice-Hall.

French, W. L., & Bell, C. (1995). *Organization development: Behavioral science interventions for organization improvement* (5th ed.). Prentice-Hall.

Freud, S. (1964). The dynamics of transference. In J. Stachey (Ed. & Trans.). *The standard edition of the complete psychological works of Sigmund Freud* (Vol. 12, pp. 97–108). Hogarth Press. (Original work published 1912)

Freud, S. (1971). Ego and the id. In J. Stachey (Ed. & Trans.). *The standard edition of the complete psychological works of Sigmund Freud* (Vol. 19, pp. 3–66). Hogarth Press. (Original work published 1923)

Freud, S. (2005). *Civilization and its discontents*. In J. Stachey (Ed. & Trans.). *The standard edition of the complete psychological works of Sigmund Freud* (Vol. 21, 2nd ed., pp. 59–144). W. W. Norton. (Original work published 1930)

Gagné, R. M. (1985). *The conditions of learning and theory of instruction* (4th ed.). Holt, Rinehart and Winston.

Gates, W. (2015). *The next outbreak we're not ready for* [Video]. Ted Conferences. https://www.ted.com/talks/bill_gates_the_next_outbreak_we_re_not_ready?language=en

Gersick, C. (1991). Revolutionary change theories: A multilevel exploration of the punctuated equilibrium paradigm. *Academy of Management Review, 16*(1), 10–36. https://doi.org/10.2307/258605

Gharajedaghi, J. (2011). *Systems thinking: Managing chaos and complexity: A platform for designing business architecture* (3rd ed.). Morgan Kaufmann.

Gibbard, G., Hartman, J., & Mann, R. (Eds.). (1974). *Analysis of groups*. Jossey-Bass.

Gladwell, M. (2000). *The tipping point: How little things can make a big difference*. Little, Brown & Company.

Golembiewski, A., & Blumberg, R. (1970). *Sensitivity training and the laboratory approach: Reading about concepts and applications* (2nd ed.). FE Peacock Publishers.

Golembiewski, R. T. (1972). *Renewing organizations: The laboratory approach to planned change*. F. E. Peacock Publications.

Google. (n.d.). *Google's vision and mission*. https://docs.google.com/document/preview?hgd=1&id=1kRYwyq6ypHxvRWaNWHFro3U8MEtOmepgi3UGrTLyCis

Greenwood, D. J., & Levin, M. (1998). *Introduction to action research: Social research for social change*. Sage Publications.

Haley, J. (1976). *Problem solving therapy*. Jossey-Bass.

Hamel, G., Prahalad, C. K., Thomas, H., & O'Neal, D. (Eds.). (1999). *Strategic flexibility: Managing in a turbulent environment*. John Wiley & Sons.

Hannan, M. T., & Freeman, J. H. (1984). Structural inertia and organizational change. *American Sociological Review, 49*(2), 149–164. https://doi.org/10.2307/2095567

Hansell, N. (1976). *The person-in-distress: On the biosocial dynamics of adaptation*. Human Sciences Press.

Herzberg, F. (2003). One more time: How do you motivate employees? *The Best of Harvard Business Review*. https://hbr.org/2003/01/one-more-time-how-do-you-motivate-employees

Hirschhorn, L. (1988). *The workplace within*. MIT Press. https://doi.org/10.7551/mitpress/7306.001.0001

Hunter, D., Bailey, A., & Taylor, B. (1995). *The art of facilitation: How to create group synergy*. Fisher Books.

Ishikawa, K. (1980). *General principles of the QC Circle*. QC Circle Headquarters, Union of Japanese Scientists and Engineers.

James, W. (1950). *Principles of psychology: Vol. 1*. Dover Publications. (Original work published 1890)

Jung, C. G. (1971). Psychological types. In R. F. Hull (Ed.), *The collected works of C.G. Jung: Vol. 6* (H. G. Baynes, Trans.). Princeton University Press. (Original work published 1921)

Kanter, R. M. (1983). *The change masters*. Simon & Schuster.

Katz, D., & Kahn, R. L. (1952). Some recent findings in human relations research in industry. In G. W. Swanson, T. M. Newcomb, & E. L. Hartley (Eds.), *Readings in social psychology* (2nd ed., pp. 650–665). Henry Holt.

Katz, D., & Kahn, R. L. (1978). *The social psychology of organizations*. John Wiley & Sons.

Katzell, R. (1960). *An action research program for organizational improvement (in Esso Standard Oil Company)*. Foundation for Research on Human Behavior.

Kelly, C. (1997, September). David Kolb, the theory of experiential learning and ESL. *The Internet TESL Journal, III*(9). https://scholar.google.com/scholar?q=David+Kolb,+The+Theory+of+Experiential+Learning+and+ESL+Curtis+Kelly&hl=en&as_sdt=0&as_vis=1&oi=cholar

Kets de Vries, M. (2006). *The leader on the couch: A clinical approach to changing people and organizations*. Jossey-Bass.

Kilburg, R. R. (1995). Integrating psychodynamic and systems theories in OD practice. *Consulting Psychology Journal, 47*(1), 28–55. https://doi.org/10.1037/1061-4087.47.1.28

Kilburg, R. R. (2000). *Executive coaching: Developing managerial wisdom in a world of chaos*. American Psychological Association. https://doi.org/10.1037/10355-000

Kilburg, R. R. (2004). When shadows fall: Using psychodynamic approaches in executive coaching. *Consulting Psychology Journal, 56*(4), 246–268. https://doi.org/10.1037/1065-9293.56.4.246

Kilburg, R. R. (2006). *Executive wisdom: Coaching and the emergence of virtuous leaders*. American Psychological Association. https://doi.org/10.1037/11464-000

Kilburg, R. R. (2020). Gender power and the psychodynamics of envy in leadership. *The Psychologist Manager Journal, 23*(3-4), 206–229. https://doi.org/10.1037/mgr0000105

Kilburg, R. R., Stokes, E. J., & Kuruvilla, C. (1998). Toward a conceptual model of organizational regression. *Consulting Psychology Journal, 50*(2), 101–119. https://doi.org/10.1037/1061-4087.50.2.101

Klein, M. (1975a). *Envy and gratitude and other works 1946–1963*. The Free Press.

Klein, M. (1975b). *Love, guilt, and reparation and other works 1921–1945*. The Free Press.

Klein, M., & Riviere, J. (1964). *Love, hate, and reparation*. W. W. Norton.

Kolb, A. Y., & Kolb, D. A. (2005). *The Kolb Learning Style Inventory—Version 3.1. 2005 technical specifications*. Hay Group/Korn Ferry.

Kolb, D. (1984). *Experiential learning: Experience as the source of learning and development*. Prentice Hall.

Kotter, J. P. (1996). *Leading change*. Harvard Business Press.

Kotter, J. P. (2012). *Leading change* (Rev. ed.). Harvard Business Press.

Kuhn, A. (1972). *The logic of social systems: A unified, deductive, system-based approach to social science*. Jossey-Bass.

Kuhn, A., & Beam, R. A. (1982). *The logic of organization: A system-based social science framework for organization theory*. Jossey-Bass.

Kuhn, T. S. (1996). *The structure of scientific revolutions* (3rd ed.). University of Chicago Press. (Original work published 1962)

Langs, R. (1976). *The bipersonal field*. Jason Aronson.

Lawrence, P. R. (2010). *Driven to lead: Good, bad, and misguided leadership*. Jossey-Bass.

Lawrence, P. R., & Lorsch, J. W. (1969). *Organization and environment: Managing differentiation and integration*. Richard D. Irwin.

Lawrence, P. R., & Nohria, N. (2002). *Driven: How human nature shapes our choices*. Jossey-Bass.

Leonard, D. C. (2002). *Learning theories: A to Z*. Greenwood Publishing Group.

Leonard, H. S. (2013). The history and current status of organizational and systems change. In H. S. Leonard, R. Lewis, A. M. Freedman, & J. Passmore (Eds.), *The Wiley-Blackwell handbook of the psychology of leadership, change, and organizational development* (pp. 239–266). Wiley-Blackwell UK. https://doi.org/10.1002/9781118326404.ch12

Leonard, H. S. (2015). Understanding the causal path between action, learning, and solutions: Maximizing the power of action learning to achieve great results.

Action Learning Research and Practice, *12*(1), 22–36. https://doi.org/10.1080/14767333.2014.977222

Leonard, H. S., & Freedman, A. M. (2013). *Great solutions through action learning: Success every time*. Learning Thru Action Press.

Leonard, H. S., & Goff, M. (2003). Leadership development as an intervention for organizational transformation: A case study. *Consulting Psychology Journal*, *55*(1), 58–67. https://doi.org/10.1037/1061-4087.55.1.58

Leonard, H. S., & Hill, C. (2021). *Leader lab: An organizational simulation for leadership development*. Learning Thru Action.

Leonard, H. S., & Lang, F. (2010). Leadership development via action learning. *Advances in Developing Human Resources*, *12*(2), 225–240. https://doi.org/10.1177/1523422310367800

Levinson, H. (2002). *Organizational assessment: A step-by-step guide to effective consulting*. American Psychological Association. https://doi.org/10.1037/10453-000

Levinson, H. (2006). *Harry Levenson on the psychology of leadership*. Harvard Business Press.

Lewin, K. Z. (1943). Defining the "field at a given time." *Psychological Review*, *50*(3), 292–310. https://doi.org/10.1037/h0062738

Lewin, K. Z. (1946). Action research and minority problems. *Journal of Social Issues*, *2*(4), 34–46. https://doi.org/10.1111/j.1540-4560.1946.tb02295.x

Lewin, K. Z. (1947). Group decision and social change. In T. M. Newcomb & E. L. Hartley (Eds.), *Readings in social psychology* (pp. 340–344). Henry Holt and Co.

Lewin, K. Z. (1948). *Resolving social conflicts: Selected papers on group dynamics*. Harper & Row.

Lewin, K. Z. (1951). *Field theory in social science: Selected papers by Kurt Lewin* (D. Cartwright, Ed.). The University of Chicago Press.

Lewin, K. Z., & Gold, M. (Eds.). (1999). *The complete social scientist: A Kurt Lewin reader*. American Psychological Association.

Likert, R. (1967). *The human organization: Its management and value*. McGraw-Hill.

Lines, R. (2004). The influence of participation in strategic change: Resistance, organizational commitment and change goal achievement. *Journal of Change Management*, *4*(3), 193–215. https://doi.org/10.1080/1469701042000221696

Lingiardi, V., & McWilliams, N. (2017). *Psychodynamic diagnostic manual* (2nd ed.). Guilford Press.

Lippitt, G. (1969). *Organizational renewal: Achieving viability in a changing world*. Appleton-Century-Crofts.

Lippitt, G., & Lippitt, R. (1986). *The consulting process in action*. University Assoc.

Lorenz, E. N. (1963). Deterministic non-periodic flow. *Journal of the Atmospheric Sciences, 20*(2), 130–141. https://doi.org/10.1175/1520-0469(1963)020<0130:DNF>2.0.CO;2

Loyd, S. (2007). *Sam Loyd's cyclopedia of 5000 puzzles, tricks, and conundrums with answers.* Ishi Press. (Original work published 1914)

Margerison, C. (2003). *Memories of Reg Revans—1907–2003.* International Management Centres Association. https://www.globalforum-actionlearning.com/index.php/about-globalforum/resources/articles/39-revans-by-margerison-memories-of-reg-revans-copy/file

Marquardt, M. J. (1999). *Action Learning in action: Transforming problems and people for world class organizational learning.* Davies-Black Publishing.

Marquardt, M. J. (2011). *Building the learning organization: Achieving strategic advantage through a commitment to learning.* Nicholas Brealey Publishing.

Marquardt, M. J., Banks, S., Cauweiler, P., & Ng, C. S. (2018). *Optimizing the power of Action Learning: Real-time strategies for developing leaders, building teams, and transforming organizations* (3rd ed.). Nicholas Brealey Publishing.

Marquardt, M. J., Leonard, H. S., Freedman, A. M., & Hill, C. C. (2009). *Action Learning for developing leaders and organizations: Principles, strategies, and cases.* American Psychological Association. https://doi.org/10.1037/11874-000

Marrow, A. J. (1967). Events leading to the establishment of the national training laboratories. *The Journal of Applied Behavioral Science, 3*(2), 144–150. https://doi.org/10.1177/002188636700300204

Marrow, A. J. (1969). *The practical theorist: The life and work of Kurt Lewin.* Basic Books.

Marshak, R. J. (2006). *Covert processes at work: Managing the five hidden dimensions of organizational change.* Barrett-Koehler.

Marsick, V. J., & Watkins, K. E. (2001). Informal and incidental learning. *New Directions for Adult and Continuing Education, 2001*(89), 25–34. https://doi.org/10.1002/ace.5

Martin, G., & Pear, J. J. (2014). *Behavior modification: What it is and how to do it* (10th ed.). Psychology Press. https://doi.org/10.4324/9781315663340

Maslow, A. H. (1954). *Motivation and personality.* HarperCollins.

Masterson, J. F. (1983). *Countertransference and psychotherapeutic technique: Teaching seminars on psychotherapy of the borderline adult.* Bruner/Mazel.

Mayo, E. (1949). *Hawthorne and the Western Electric Company: The social problems of an industrial civilisation.* Routledge Books.

McGregor, D. (1960). *The human side of enterprise.* McGraw-Hill.

McLean, G. N. (2005). *Organization development: Principles, processes, performance.* Barrett-Koehler Publishers.

Media, F. (2019). *Ford makes leadership changes as it speeds transformation.* https://media.ford.com/content/fordmedia/fna/us/en/news/2019/04/10/ford-makes-leadership-changes-as-it-speeds-transformation.html

Milgram, S. (1974). *Obedience to authority: An experimental view.* Harper & Row.

Miller, J. C. (1955). Toward a general theory for the behavioral sciences. *American Psychologist, 10*(9), 513–531. https://doi.org/10.1037/h0045498

Minuchin, S. (1974). *Families and family therapy.* Harvard University Press. https://doi.org/10.4159/9780674041127

Nadler, D. A., & Tushman, M. L. (1995). *Types of organizational change: From incremental improvements to discontinuous transformation.* Jossey-Bass.

Newton, I. (1999). *Principia: Mathematical principles of natural philosophy* (I. B. Cohen, A. Whitman, & J. Budenz, Trans.). University of California Press. (Original work published 1726)

Nisbet, R. A. (1967). *The sociological tradition.* Heinemann Educational Books.

Niu, D. (2021). *Careercation.* https://www.tinypulse.com/careercation

Oliver, C. (1991). Strategic responses to institutional processes. *Academy of Management Review, 16*(1), 145–179. https://doi.org/10.2307/258610

Oshry, B. (2007). *Seeing systems: Unlocking the mysteries of organizational life* (2nd ed.). Berrett-Koehler.

Palazzoli, M. (1978). *Paradox and counterparadox: A new model in the therapy of the family in schizophrenic transaction.* Rowman & Littlefield Publishers.

Pasmore, W. A. (2011). Tipping the balance: Overcoming persistent problems in organizational change. In A. Shani, R. Woodman, & W. Pasmore (Eds.), *Research in organizational change and development* (Vol. 19, pp. 259–292). JAI Press. https://doi.org/10.1108/S0897-3016(2011)0000019011

Patten, T. H. (1981). *Organization development through teambuilding.* John Wiley & Sons.

Patton, M. Q. (2002). *Qualitative research & evaluation methods* (3rd ed.). Sage Publications.

Pavlov, I. V. (1927). *Conditioned reflexes.* Oxford University Press.

Pfeiffer, J. W., & Jones, J. E. (Eds.). (1969–1986). *The annual handbooks for group facilitators.* University Associates Publishers and Consultants.

Piaget, J. (1965). *The moral development of the child.* The Free Press.

Pinker, S. (1994). On language. *Journal of Cognitive Neuroscience, 6*(1), 92–98. https://doi.org/10.1162/jocn.1994.6.1.92

Pinker, S. (1997). *How the mind works.* W. W. Norton & Co.

Plato. (2013). *The Republic and other dialogues.* Barnes and Noble. (Original work published ca. 375 BCE)

Prochaska, J. O., & DiClemente, C. C. (1994). *The transtheoretical approach: Crossing traditional boundaries of therapy.* Krieger Publishing Co.

Prochaska, J. O., & Norcross, J. C. (2002). Stages of change. In J. C. Norcross (Ed.), *Psychotherapy relationships that work* (pp. 303–313). Oxford University Press.

Quinn, J. G. (1980). Managing strategic change. *Sloan Management Review, 22*(4), 3–20.

Rachman, S. (1997). The evolution of cognitive behavior therapy. In D. M. Clark & C. B. Fairburn (Eds.), *Science and practice of cognitive behavior therapy* (pp. 3–26). Oxford University Press.

Racker, H. (1968). *Transference and countertransference.* International Universities Press.

Rapoport, A. (1956). The diffusion problem in mass behavior. *General Systems Yearbook, 1*, 6.

Revans, R. W. (1982). *The origins and growth of Action Learning.* Chartwell-Brat.

Revans, R. W. (1983). *The ABC's of Action Learning.* Chartwell-Brat.

Revans, R. W. (1984). *Action Learning—Introduction by Reg Revans.* International Foundation for Action Learning. https://www.youtube.com/watch?v=2bJ9RXkYPSU

Revans, R. W. (1991). *On intellect and wisdom* [Video]. Global University for Lifelong Learning. https://www.youtube.com/watch?v=J2D_sGQcVz8

Rock, D. (2009). *Your brain at work: Strategies for overcoming distraction, regaining focus, and working smarter all day long.* Harper Business.

Rock, D., & Page, L. J. (2009). *Coaching with the brain in mind: Foundations for practice.* Wiley.

Rogers, C. (1965a). *Client-centered therapy.* Houghton Mifflin.

Rogers, C. (1965b). Dealing with psychological tensions. *The Journal of Applied Behavioral Science, 1*(1), 6–24. https://doi.org/10.1177/002188636500100103

Rogers, C. (1970). *On encounter groups.* Harrow Books/Harper and Row.

Ruma, S. (1974). A diagnostic model for organizational change: Where the flexible is functional. *Social Change, 1*(4), 4.

Sawyer, T. L., & Deering, S. (2013). Adaptation of the US Army's After-Action Review for simulation debriefing in healthcare. *Simulation in Healthcare, 8*(6), 388–397. https://doi.org/10.1097/SIH.0b013e31829ac85c

Schachter, S., Ellertson, N., McBride, D., & Gregory, D. (1951). An experimental study of cohesiveness and productivity. *Human Relations, 4*(3), 229–238. https://doi.org/10.1177/001872675100400303

Schaffer, R. H., & Thomson, H. A. (1992). Successful change programs begin with results. *Harvard Business Review, 70*(1), 80–89.

Schein, E. H. (1996a). Culture: The missing concept in organizational studies. *Administrative Science Quarterly, 41*(2), 229–240. https://doi.org/10.2307/2393715

Schein, E. H. (1996b). Three cultures of management: The key to organizational learning. *MIT Sloan Management Review, 38*(1), 9–20.

Schein, E. H. (1999). *Process consultation revisited: Building the helping relationship*. Addison Wesley.

Schumpeter, J. A. (1942/1975). *Capitalism, socialism and democracy*. Harper & Row.

Schwarz, R. (2002). *The skilled facilitator: A comprehensive resource for consultants, facilitators, managers, trainers, and coaches*. Jossey-Bass.

Segal, T. (2020). *Troubled Asset Relief Program (TARP)*. https://www.investopedia.com/terms/t/troubled-asset-relief-program-tarp.asp

Seligman, M. E. P. (1998). American Psychological Association 1998 Presidential Address. https://www.apa.org/about/governance/president/address

Seligman, M. E. P. (2002). *Authentic happiness: Using the new positive psychology to realize your potential for lasting fulfillment*. Free Press.

Seligman, M. E. P., & Csikszentmihalyi, M. (2000). Positive psychology. An introduction. *American Psychologist*, *55*(1), 5–14. https://doi.org/10.1037/0003-066X.55.1.5

Senge, P. (1990). *The fifth discipline: The art & science of the learning organization*. Currency & Doubleday.

Shepard, H. A. (1960). An Action-Research model. In *Action Research program for organization improvement*. The Foundation for Research on Human Behavior, University of Michigan.

Sherer, P. D., & Lee, K. (2002). Institutional change in large law firms: A resource dependency and institutional perspective. *Academy of Management Journal*, *45*(1), 102–119.

Smith, A. (2003). *The wealth of nations*. Bantam Classics. (Original work published 1776)

Snyder, C. R., & Lopez, S. J. (2001). *Handbook of positive psychology*. Oxford University Press.

Spector, B., & Beer, M. (1994). Beyond TQM programmes. *Journal of Organizational Change Management*, *7*(2), 63–70. https://doi.org/10.1108/09534819410056087

Stacey, R. D. (1992). *Managing the unknowable: Strategic boundaries between order and chaos in organizations*. Jossey-Bass.

Stacey, R. D., Griffin, D., & Shaw, P. (2000). *Complexity and management: Fad or radical challenge to systems thinking?* Routledge.

Starbuck, W. (1971). *Organizational growth and development*. Blackwell.

Taylor, F. (2011). *The principles of scientific management*. Forgotten Books.

Thelen, H. A. (1954). *Dynamics of groups at work*. University of Chicago Press.

Thompson, J. D. (1967). *Organizations in action*. McGraw-Hill.

Tolman, C. W., Cherry, F., Van Hezewijk, R., & Lubek, I. (1995). *Problems of theoretical psychology*. Captus Press.

Tuckman, B. W. (1965). Developmental sequences in small groups. *Psychological Bulletin*, *63*(6), 384–399. https://doi.org/10.1037/h0022100

Tushman, M. L., & Romanelli, E. (1985). Organizational evolution: A metamorphosis model of convergence and reorientation. In L. Cummings & B. Staw (Eds.), *Research in organizational behavior* (Vol. 7, pp. 171–222). JAI Press.

Useem, J. (2019, August). The stock-buyback swindle. *The Atlantic*. https://www.theatlantic.com/magazine/archive/2019/08/the-stock-buyback-swindle/592774/

Vaill, P. (1996). *Learning as a way of being: Strategies for survival in a world of permanent white water*. Jossey-Bass.

Van de Ven, A., & Poole, M. S. (1995). Explaining development and change in organizations. *Academy of Management Review, 20*(3), 510–540. https://doi.org/10.5465/amr.1995.9508080329

von Bertalanffy, L. (1950). An outline of general system theory. *British Journal for the Philosophy of Science, 1*, 134–165. https://doi.org/10.1093/bjps/I.2.134

von Bertalanffy, L. (1969). *General system theory*. George Braziller.

Watkins, K. E., & Marsick, V. J. (1992a). Building the learning organization: A new role for human resource developers. *Studies in Continuing Education, 14*(2), 115–129. https://doi.org/10.1080/0158037920140203

Watkins, K. E., & Marsick, V. J. (1992b). Towards a theory of informal and incidental learning in organizations. *International Journal of Lifelong Education, 11*(4), 287–300. https://doi.org/10.1080/0260137920110403

Watson, J. B. (1930). *Behaviorism* (Rev. ed.). W. W. Norton & Co.

Watzlawick, P., Weakland, J. H., & Fisch, R. (1974). *Change: Principles of problem formation and problem resolution*. W. W. Norton & Co.

Weber, M. (2021). *The theory of social and economic organization* (A. M. Henderson & T. Parsons, Eds.). Martino Publishing. (Original work published 1921)

Weick, K. E. (1995). *Sensemaking in organizations*. Sage Publications.

Weick, K. E. (2001). *Making sense of the organization* (Vols. 1 & 2). Blackwell.

Wheatley, M. J. (2006). *Leadership and the new science: Discovering order in a chaotic world*. (3rd ed.). Berritt-Koehler Publishers.

Wheelwright, P. (1959). *Heraclitus*. Princeton University Press.

Wilhelm, H. (1960). *Change: Eight lectures on the I Ching* (C. F. Baynes, Trans.). Harper Torchbooks.

Wilson, E. O. (1998). *Consilience: The unity of knowledge*. Knopf.

Wood, W., & Rünger, D. (2016). Psychology of habit. *Annual Review of Psychology, 67*(1), 289–314. https://doi.org/10.1146/annurev-psych-122414-033417

Wurmser, L. (2007). *Torment me, but don't abandon me: Psychoanalysis of the severe neuroses in a new key*. Jason Aronson.

Index

About the Authors

H. Skipton Leonard, PhD, is managing director of Learning Thru Action, LLC. Trained as a social and organizational psychologist, Dr. Leonard has devoted his career to helping individuals, teams, and organizations achieve their goals and accomplish their missions by learning how to be more adaptive, creative, and innovative. Dr. Leonard received his doctoral and undergraduate degrees in psychology from New York University and Middlebury College, respectively. He is a licensed psychologist in the state of Virginia and served his country as an officer in the U.S. Army. Prior to his current position, he was a vice president and executive consultant with Personnel Decisions International (now PDI Ninth House-Korn Ferry). Dr. Leonard has consulted with numerous Fortune 500 and Global 1000 companies, such as Pfizer, Microsoft, Target, Wells Fargo, American Express, AstraZeneca, Boeing, Bechtel, Daimler Chrysler, Dell, NCS-Pearson, and SAIC. He also has experience with NGOs such as the IMF and World Bank as well as U.S. government organizations such as the National Institutes of Health, U.S. Army, U.S. Postal Service, General Services Administration, U.S. Department of Agriculture, and Government Accounting Office. Dr. Leonard has been a faculty member at a number of top universities, including the Carey School of Business at Johns Hopkins University, the Department of Human and Organizational Learning at George Washington University, the School of Public Policy at American University, the Graduate Department of Psychology at George Mason University, and the State University of New York at Plattsburgh. A leader in his profession, Dr. Leonard is a fellow in the American Psychological Association and the Society of Consulting Psychology and is past president of the Society of Consulting Psychology. He was also the founding editor of a peer-reviewed journal, *Consulting Psychology Journal.* He has more than 100 books, book chapters, articles, and professional presentations to his credit.

Richard R. Kilburg, PhD, is widely recognized as a leader in the field of executive coaching and development, a field that he has written and lectured about extensively for 25 years. Dr. Kilburg has provided consultation and executive and leadership coaching in many well-known private, public sector, health, and educational organizations, including Glaxo Smith Klein, Reebok, Bell/Riddell Sports, INOVA Health Systems, Human Genome Sciences, Johns Hopkins University, the University of Utah Medical Sciences Center, Vanderbilt University School of Medicine, and Westinghouse Health Systems. He received his PhD in clinical and community psychology from the University of Pittsburgh and received postgraduate training in mental health administration from Harvard University. He has held teaching positions at Johns Hopkins University (JHU), the University of Pittsburgh, and Carnegie-Mellon University. Dr. Kilburg was instrumental in developing and directing the Organization Development program within the Carey Business School at JHU. In recent years, he has been a principal at RRK Coaching and Executive Development, providing coaching and other development services to senior leaders around the world. In addition to being selected as a fellow by the American Psychological Association and the Society of Consulting Psychology, Dr. Kilburg was the founding president of the Society of Psychologists in Management. He has received numerous awards for his scholarship and thought leadership, including for Distinguished Contribution to the Society of Psychologists in Management, the Harry and Miriam Levinson Award for Outstanding Contributions to Consulting Psychology, the Elliott Jacques Memorial Publication Award (thrice), the Vision of Excellence Award from the Institute of Coaching, and the RHR International Award for Excellence in Consulting Psychology. Dr. Kilburg is the author of six books, 57 articles and book chapters, and many dozens of professional presentations.

Arthur M. Freedman, MBA, PhD, was considered a thought and practice leader in organization development, consultation, and Action Learning. Dr. Freedman consulted with dozens of leading corporations, nonprofit organizations, and governmental organizations throughout the world, including Microsoft, Mercedes-Benz, Coopers & Lybrand, the Ministry of Atomic Energy (Russia), National Education Association, Boston Consulting Group, ADP, Gordon Institute of Business (South Africa), Southern California Edison, Veterans Administration, the U.S. Defense Intelligence Agency, the National Institutes of Health, the Houston Police Department, and Kaiser Permanente. Most recently, Dr. Freedman served as adjunct faculty in the Carey Business School at Johns Hopkins University. He was a visiting scholar at the Center for Organizational Dynamics, University of Pennsylvania. Dr. Freedman earned both his BS and his MBA at Boston University's College of Business Administration and his PhD in personality and clinical psychology at the University of Chicago. He was a fellow of the American Psychological Association and the Society of Consulting Psychology. He received many prestigious awards: the 1994 RHR International Award for Excellence in Consulting Psychology; 2007 Harry and Miriam Levinson Award for Exceptional Contributions to Organizational Consulting Psychology; Hall of Fame Award from the National Hispanic Institute in 2011; 2012 Distinguished Psychologist in Management award from the Society of Psychologists in Management; and Elliott Jaques Award for the outstanding *Consulting Psychology Journal* article of 1997. In addition, Dr. Freedman was an executive board member for the World Institute for Action Learning. A prolific author and presenter, he produced more than 125 books, book chapters, articles, and professional presentations.